Read On!

FOUNDATION

by
Susan Davies

Heinemann Educational,
a division of Heinemann Educational Books Ltd,
Halley Court, Jordan Hill, Oxford OX2 8EJ

OXFORD LONDON EDINBURGH
MELBOURNE SYDNEY AUCKLAND
IBADAN NAIROBI GABORONE HARARE
KINGSTON PORTSMOUTH NH (USA)
SINGAPORE MADRID BOLOGNA ATHENS

Copyright © 1991 Susan Davies
First published 1991

British Library Cataloguing in Publicaion Data
Davies, Susan, 1957 -
Read on!
KS3
1 Secondary schools. Students. Reading Skills. Development
I Title
428.430712

ISBN 0 435 10286 9

Cover Design *The Design Revolution ·Brighton*
Designed by *The Design Revolution ·Brighton*

Printed in Great Britain by *Thomson Litho, East Kilbride, Scotland.*

dedication

For Rachael
whose happy laugh brightens even rainy days.

With love Mum

INTRODUCTION

When I wrote **Read On!** I had three aims in mind. First, to provide the classroom teacher with a range of reading material that would help to fulfil the demands made by profile component 2 of the National Curriculum in English. Second, that this material would be interesting and fun for both teacher and pupil alike. Third, that the material and assignments would enable pupils at the earliest age to acquire the skills they would need later on in their school life.

The reading component of the National Curriculum is demanding. It expects teachers to provide students with passages taken from prose, drama and poetry from across the centuries. At the same time teachers must not forget the non-literary use of language by the media, in advertising and news reports. Teachers are also expected to provide pupils with the opportunities to develop their reference skills and understanding of materials from other curriculum areas. If at this point you are worried about gathering this breadth of material, you need look no further than the contents list for **Read On!** It is all there for you – extracts from pantomime to *Macbeth*, from *The Monster Garden* to *Frankenstein*, advertising and newspapers, recipes and instructions on how to make a paper dart. But most of all, the material is suited to the age and varying ability of students and is already tried and tested in the classroom.

The **Focus On**... sections at the beginning of each chapter provide students with information about the type of reading activity covered in the chapter. Teachers, a community policeman and the school cleaner talk about their reasons for reading a newspaper. Students explain why they read and how they choose a book. Gillian Clarke, poet, and Greg Cullen, writer, explain why poetry and drama are important as writing forms.

Read On! helps pupils to think about why they are reading and what they can gain from the activity. Similarly it helps them to recognize that the reason for reading very often determines the way in which we read – the differences between scanning a newspaper for information and reading between the lines of a poem for instance.

Finally, **Read On!** is more than just another comprehension book for National Curriculum. It allows pupils to respond to texts in a number of different ways, sometimes by engaging with the language used, sometimes by responding to the contents of the text but always in a manner that enables pupils to write for a variety of purposes. Thus, Read **On!** should enable teachers who are always short of actual teaching and classroom time to cover many of the demands made by the writing component of the National Curriculum. In the same way the oral activities in **Read On!** provide opportunities for speaking and listening. So, while focusing primarily on reading, **Read On!** allows an intergrated approach to all the profile components of the National Curriculum in English.

CONTENTS

	Introduction	iii
	Skills Matrix	vi
1	Focus on Advertising	8
1.1	Words and pictures	10
1.2	Attracting attention	14
2	Focus on Reading for Information	18
2.1	A trio of tortoise tales	22
2.2	Acid rain	24
3	Focus on Following Instructions	28
3.1	Using a recipe	30
3.2	Making a papier mâché model	32
3.3	Craft design	36
4	Focus on Reference Skills	38
4.1	Using a book	40
4.2	Finding your way around a book	41
4.3	Using a dictionary	42
5	Focus on Selecting Information	44
5.1	Planning a holiday	48

5.2	Designing a tourist Brochure	58
6	Focus on Reading Pictures	60
6.1	Macbeth	62
7	Focus on Drama	66
7.1	Pantomime	68
8	Focus on Poetry	74
8.1	Poetry and posters	76
8.2	Uncle Edward	80
8.3	Pictures in words	82
8.4	Haiku	84
8.5	Inventing words	86
9	Focus on Fiction	88
9.1	Conrad the factory made boy	92
9.2	Summer's end	96
9.3	The sheep-pig	98
9.4	Madam Doubtfire	102
9.5	Making monsters (1)	110
9.6	Making monsters (2)	116
9.7	Alice in Wonderland	118
9.8	M13 on form	122

Skills Matrix - *Reading Profile Component*

Unit No.	Strand 1 *Fluency / Range*			Strand 2 *Response*		
	3/4	5/6	7	3/4	5/6	7
Section 1						
1.1						
1.2						
1.3						
Section 2						
2.1						
2.2						
Section 3						
3.1						
3.2						
3.3						
Section 4						
4.1						
4.2						
Section 5						
5.1						
5.2						
Section 6						
6.1	●	●	●	●	●	●
Section 7						
7.1	●	●			●	
Section 8						
8.1	●	●		●	●	●
8.2	●	●		●	●	
8.3	●	●		●	●	●
8.4	●	●				
8.5	●	●	●	●	●	
Section 9						
9.1	●	●		●	●	
9.2	●	●	●	●	●	●
9.3	●	●		●	●	●
9.4	●	●		●	●	●
9.5	●	●	●	●	●	●
9.6		●	●			
9.7	●	●	●	●	●	

Strand 3 Media / Nonlit			Strand 4 Study Skills			Strand 5 Knowledge about Language		
3/4	5/6	7	3/4	5/6	7	3/4	5/6	7
	●	●					●	
	●	●					●	●
		●					●	
	●	●					●	●
	●	●					●	
			●	●	●			
				●	●			
			●	●				
			●					
			●					
			●	●	●			
	●		●	●	●			
							●	
							●	
								●
								●
								●
							●	●
							●	
							●	●
							●	●
	●							

FOCUS ON Advertising

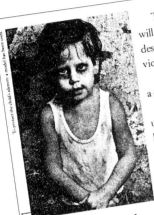

This Christmas the NSPCC will be helping many frightened, desperate children who are the victims of neglect.

£20.66 can begin to protect a child from abuse.

If you can send us that sum, using the coupon below we know of plenty of children who, for the first time in their lives would like to say 'Thanks, Santa.'

For this lonely, neglected little boy Father Christmas exists. If you've got £20.66 to spare, it's you.

▼ **Assignment 1**

Look carefully at the advertisements on these two pages.
1 Who is advertising and what are they advertising?
2 Make a list of the places you would expect to find advertising like this.
3 An advertisement is supposed to capture your attention. How does each of these advertisements try to attract you?
4 Do they succeed?

FOR 3 DAYS THE ONLY SHOTS IN THE LEBANON CAME FROM UNICEF.

In September, UNICEF arranged a ceasefire in the Lebanon.

Over 3 days we vaccinated 350,000 children against such potentially lethal diseases as polio, tetanus and diptheria.

And then we repeated the operation in the next two months.

We've organised the very same thing in the El Salvador war for the past three years.

But in developing countries across the world, 15 million children still die every year before the age of 5 from preventable diseases and malnutrition.

We can drastically reduce this appalling figure by helping these countries educate parents in simple health and nutrition programmes.

By immunization alone, we can eradicate six fatal diseases within the next three years.

Inevitably, waging this kind of war costs money.

And all our income, whether from governments or individuals, is entirely voluntary.

Please ring 01-200 0200 now, or fill in the coupon and give us as much ammunition as you can afford.

UNICEF UK
Children count on us. We count on you

Advertising

IF AN ADVERT IS WRONG, WHO PUTS IT RIGHT?

We do. The Advertising Standards Authority ensures advertisements meet with the strict Code of Advertising Practice.

So if you question an advertiser, they have to answer to us.

To find out more about the ASA, please write to Advertising Standards Authority, Department X, Brook House, Torrington Place, London WC1E 7HN.

ASA

This space is donated in the interests of high standards in advertisements.

SUPERB ACTIVITY HOLIDAYS
for Children & Teenagers

PGL Adventure Holidays are action packed from breakfast to bedtime. They're fantastic fun for kids. Safe and sound for parents.
- Over 70 great activities from motorsports to watersports, pony trekking to abseiling
- More than 20 centres, UK and abroad
- Separate holidays for each age group
- Caring supervision on a 1:5 ratio
- Friendly instruction and excellent equipment
- Approved by major activity associations

FANTASTIC FUN SAFE & SOUND
33 YEARS EXPERIENCE

ABTA 46875

☐ Please send us a free copy of PGL's Children and Teenage Adventure brochure.
☐ Mum and Dad are interested in joining too, please send details of the separate Family Adventure Holidays.

Name: _____ Address: _____

Postcode: _____
PGL Adventure Holidays, 322 Station Street, Ross-on-Wye, HR9 7AH.
☎ **(0989) 763511/ 764211 (24 hrs)**

25,000 ELEPHANTS TO BE KILLED IN THE NEXT 3 MONTHS

On October 9th the world finally meets to decide whether the African elephant should be lawfully protected as an "endangered species". But, between now and then, another 25,000 elephants will be slaughtered for ivory ● Isn't that reason enough to add your name to the thousands of signatures we need to prevent the elephant becoming a memory?

Please add this signature to your IVORY pledge and send me more information.

Signature _____

I'd also like to donate £ _____ E25K/1

Elefriends, 162 Boundaries Road, London SW12 8HG.
___-202. (25p cheap, 38p peak per min.)

ELEFRIENDS

Words and Pictures

▼ **Assignment 1**

Look at these advertisements carefully. Then answer the following questions about each:
1. Who is advertising and why?
2. What are the pictures of?
3. Why do you think the designer has included these pictures?
4. What do you think of them, and what effect do they have on you?
5. If you do not like either of the pictures, suggest another you would have used.

IN OUR COUNTRY MILLIONS OF CHILDREN GET MEASLES.

IN SOME COUNTRIES MEASLES GETS MILLIONS OF CHILDREN.

You can't imagine anybody in Britain dying from measles. We overcame that problem a long time ago.

But the reality is that in developing countries it still kills 2 million children every year.

Deaths which UNICEF could prevent. Two simple vaccinations will give a child immunity to measles and five other potentially lethal diseases.

They cost about £5 and right now we're saving over a million lives a year.

With your help we could vaccinate all the world's children by 1990.

We desperately need your donation, because all our income is voluntary, whether it's from governments or individuals.

Please ring 01-200 0200 now or fill in the coupon and send as much as you can afford.

Just £5 will save a child's life. Who could be immune to that?

UNICEF UK
Children count on us. We count on you.

Would you be more inclined to help a battered child if he stopped you in the street?

The answer is probably yes.

But a battered and bruised child is a rare public sight. Child abuse is committed behind closed doors.

It's a private crime needing public awareness if anything is to be done to stop it.

It's a crime that on the surface knows no reason.

Why did a mother let her nine month old baby son starve to within hours of death?

Why did a father sexually abuse his daughter for five years?

And why was an 8 year old boy beaten by his parents who then stubbed out cigarettes on his arms?

Some of the solutions can be provided by the NSPCC.

We have highly trained staff that, once made aware of these private crimes, can do something about them.

We can send a Child Protection Officer to help children who are in danger.

We can counsel parents to help stop abuse happening again.

We can do something about the estimated 3 or 4 children that are dying from abuse each week.

You may never see them. But you can help them.

Sending £20.66 or more will pay for the first visit of an NSPCC Child Protection Officer.

Assignment 2

Look at the captions. The caption is the title written above the picture.

1 How has the writer of each tried to attract your attention?
2 What do you think of the captions?
3 Which do you prefer and why?
4 Now read the information around each picture. Do you think you would have bothered to read this information if you had seen either of these posters in a magazine? Explain why or why not.
5 Try to explain which poster you prefer and why.

▼ **Assignment 1**

Many advertisers use famous people to advertise their products.
1 Why do you think they do this?
2 If you saw a product being advertised by someone you liked, would you buy it?
3 Would you be put off products if they had someone famous that you didn't like advertising them?
4 How do you think an advertiser might choose a famous person to advertise a product? Think about what different advertisers are trying to sell, and the people they are trying to sell it to.

▼ **Assignment 3**

Now look carefully at the words written at the side of the advertisement.
1 Look at the first paragraph. It mentions other famous people from other sports. Why?
2 A lot of the words or phrases here have a hidden message to try to persuade you to join this club. Here are some of the main ones, with answers alongside but in the wrong order. Try to work out the correct hidden message for each word or phrase. Are all these hidden messages true?

▼ **Assignment 2**

Now look at the words in the caption. Advertisers use words that are supposed to attract their customers.
1 What does the word 'elite' mean? How is it meant to make you feel?
2 How else does this caption try to attract your attention?
3 What is the hidden suggestion (idea) in the second part – 'your best chance of catching up with Daley Thompson'?
How does this idea fit in with the picture?

Action-packed poster
I don't want to be left out in the rush – I simply must send off now.

Rush me my membership card and gift pack
This will really look good on my wall.

Just £5.75
You will receive a really good gift in return.

Get closer to your favourite stars
It's a small amount to pay for so much

Bumper gift pack
This club will mean you can meet your favourite stars.

1:2

Attracting Attention

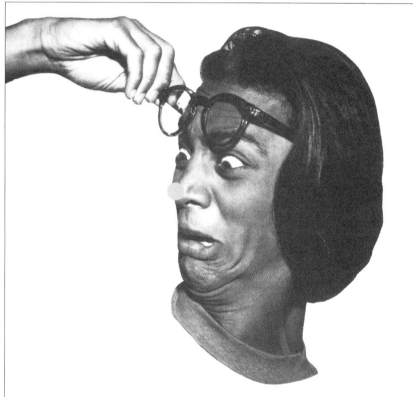

Advertising

Assignment 1

1. Look at this advertisement for Tri-ac. How does it try to attract your attention?
2. Look at the picture and the main caption. Now look at the captions used in the advertisements on the other pages. Is there anything similar about the use of language?
3. Advertisements often play with words. How have the advertisers played with words here?
4. In the Daley Thompson advertisement, the caption, the picture and the wording of the advertisement were all carefully linked together. Look at the caption, the picture and the last part of the writing here. How do all these link up?
5. Look closely at the picture. What do you think of the expression on this person's face? Do you like the picture?
6. Do you think this is a hard or an easy product to sell? Would you admit that you needed a product like this?
7. Do you find the advertisement amusing? Try to explain why, or why not.

Assignment 2

You are a group of advertising consultants and have been asked to launch an advertising campaign for three new products. The first is a hair restorer that cures baldness in men and women. The second is a cream designed to get rid of double chins. The third is a face make-up that when used daily will get rid of unwanted facial hair.

As yet the company are unsure what to call these products and want you to come up with a snappy name for each of them. They also want you to design a poster for each, complete with a caption. They have suggested that you use famous people in selling these products–though you might have some trouble persuading the famous to help you!

Assignment 1

Look at these two advertisements. You are the designers of both of them, and you have to explain to the makers of Tizer and to British Rail why you have chosen to use a chimp in one and old ladies playing bowls in another as a means of attracting young people's attention. Here are some ideas to help you:

- Young people don't like reading lots of words but like an advertisement that is all picture.

- Young people like animals.

- Chimps have been used a lot in films.

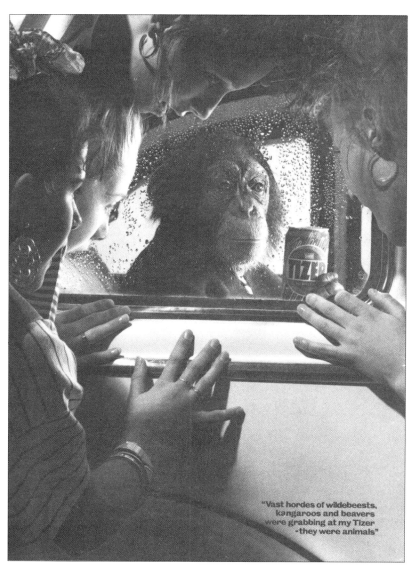

"Vast hordes of wildebeests, kangaroos and beavers were grabbing at my Tizer – they were animals"

Advertising

1. Both advertisements are funny. Where does the humour come from? Look at the captions in both.
2. When you read **'The youth of today are simply going too far!'** what does it remind you of? Do you expect the reply the advertisement gives?
3. Now write a letter to Tizer and one to British Rail to tell them why you have designed the posters this way, why you like your ideas and why you think they will work. Start your letter by describing the poster you have designed for them.

FOCUS ON
Reading for information

Most people get their information about what's happening from newspapers. How do you choose the newspaper you would like to read? How do you read a newspaper when you've chosen it? There are all sorts of different reasons for choosing a newspaper and, when you've chosen it, you might only want to read certain parts of it, rather than reading from cover to cover.

A group of students set out to discover how people working around their school in Wales chose and read their papers. They asked the following questions:

1 What newspaper do you read?
2 Which part do you read first?
3 What do you like about it?
4 Why do you read this paper in particular and how long have you been reading it?

Mrs Hughes, cleaning supervisor

1 What newspaper do you read?
> *Today.*

2 Which part do you read first?
> I start at the front and read through to the back, usually. Except the sports page.

3 What do you like about it?
> It's informative and colourful because they use coloured photos and it has things concerning children, healthy diets and conservation.

4 Why do you read this paper in particular and how long have you been reading it?
> About two years. I used to read the *Sun* but I found I might as well have read a comic because the things written in it weren't worth reading.

Reading for information

Mrs Thomas, drama teacher

1 What newspaper do you read?

The Guardian and the *Western Mail.*

The *Western Mail* – because it tells me about my locality and what's going on in Wales.

2 Which part do you read first?

The front page, the television page and, if it's *The Guardian*, I read the women's page.

3 What do you like about them?

The Guardian – I like its political angle and I like the way it thinks.

4 Why do you read this paper in particular and how long have you been reading it?

I read it because I like the style, particularly in *The Guardian*. It's funny, it's been out for a long time and I've been reading it since I was 18.

Mr Preece, PE teacher

1 What newspaper do you read?

During the week I read the *Western Mail*.

2 Which part do you read first?

I always read the front page first.

3 What do you like about it?

I like it because it's the national newspaper and it also covers local information. It's very informative, covering news of the day and foreign news. It also has information about the stock market. It covers so many things and is an excellent paper.

4 Why do you read this paper in particular and how long have you been reading it?

Well, as I said, it is local and national. I've read it since I was 15 or 16.

Reading for information

PC Morgan, local community policeman

1 What newspaper do you read?

> Well, I don't read a newspaper every day. On a day off usually I'll buy *The Times* or sometimes *The Independent*.

2 Which part do you read first?

> Well ... my main interest is music. So I tend to look through the papers for any music reviews and then I will read anything on sport that I'm interested in, and then any items of news that catch my eye.

3 What do you like about it?

> Mainly the depth it goes into with most of its reviews and its sports reports.

4 Why do you read this paper in particular and how long have you been reading it?

> Well I've been reading *The Times* I suppose for about ... fourteen years. Before being a policeman I worked in a bank and during those years I read the *Financial Times,* and I do buy that occasionally, but that's specifically for the music reviews.

▼ **Over to you**

1 In groups, make a list of the reasons people give for choosing their newspapers.
2 None of our interviewees read the whole paper. What do the bits they choose to read, or skip, tell you about their personal interests?
3 Ask people you know about the papers they read and why they read them. Can you add anything to your list of reasons above?

2:1

A TRIO OF TORTOISE TALES

Having seen how people choose and read their newspapers, we are now going to look at how newspaper articles are written. Read the articles on this page and then work on the assignments.

▼ Assignment 1

1 Look at the headlines: **'A trio of tortoise tales'** and **'Tunnel tames traffic troubles'**.

Almost all the words start with the same letter. What effect does this have when you read them aloud?

2 There is a special word for this technique of using words that start with the same letter or sound: **alliteration**. Why do you think headline writers use alliteration?

▼ Assignment 2

Now look at the way the rest of the 'Speedy' article is written.
1 What does the first short paragraph encourage you to do?
2 Why are the paragraphs short?
3 What sort of information is given? Is it all essential?
4 Why is the article split up by the heading 'Identity parade'?
5 Why do you think the writer includes words spoken by Paul?

▼ Assignment 3

Using all the tricks you've discovered for writing a news article, write your own based on the following information:

At approximately 8.30 p.m. a van was seen outside a zoo. The van driver sped off when Mrs Daymar asked if she could help. She has given a description of the van and the driver to the police.

At 10.30 p.m. a man was seen with a piece of rope outside the zoo. He was seen by a passing cyclist, Simon Rozenberg, who was going home from the local pub, 'The Cock and Bull'.

At 12.30 a.m. people who live in Northcote Road, Bristol, near the zoo, were woken by the sound of animals.

At 2.00 a.m. security guards checked the grounds. All was quiet at that time.

At 6.30 a.m. a zoo-keeper found that a yeti was missing.

Reading for information

EARLY TIMES — September 28th to October 4th, 1989 — Page 5

A trio of tortoise tales

Anne Haynes, 9, meets as heavyweight at the British Chelonia Group's London Weigh In

Speedy in police 'chase'

IN the Midlands, a teenager had to rescue his pet tortoise, Speedy, who was under arrest.

Speedy was found doing 0.1mph along the M6 on the outskirts of Birmingham by a motorway patrol sergeant. Such recklessness nearly cost the tortoise his life.

Only the sharp eyes of a lorry driver saved Speedy from being squashed. He pulled up and stopped in front of the intrepid tortoise to prevent other vehicles from running him over.

The police took him into custody for obstructing the public highway, and set about tracing his owner. Their appeal for help was so successful, they received offers of a new home from all over the country. One lady even phoned up from Australia.

Identity parade

The police decided the only way to establish who Speedy's real owner was, would be to hold an identity parade, like the ones they organise to prove who committed crimes. They got together a group of tortoises, and secretly tagged Speedy just to make sure they didn't forget which one of the group he was.

Among those who had claimed to own Speedy was Paul Dunn, 13, from Brookdale near Birmingham. He came to the ID parade and passed the test, recognising Speedy at once.

"I knew I could prove it was Speedy," said Paul, "because he has a dent in his shell. And if I breathe heavily into his face, he breathes back."

He had gone missing two weeks earlier, and walked more than a mile to the motorway. When he got home, Speedy was given his favourite feast - a bowl of bread and strawberry jam, soaked in milk.

TORTOISE owners all over the UK have been getting their pets weighed and measured recently, and for a very important reason.

This is the time when tortoises go into hibernation for the winter. But if a tortoise is underweight when it nods off there is a strong likelihood it won't wake up again.

That is why the British Chelonia Group [the word meaning reptiles which have shells] are weighing and measuring tortoises at centres all over the country, checking that tortoises are the correct weight for their size.

If you own a tortoise and would like to find out more about the British Chelonia Group you can write to: BCG, 39 Brambles Farm Drive, Hillingdon, Uxbridge, Middlesex, UB10 0DY.

Tunnel tames traffic troubles

YOU'VE heard of toad tunnels and badger tunnels to allow animals to pass safely under roads or railways. Well, here's a new one - the motorway tortoise tunnel.

Road builders have agreed to make a passage especially for the rare reptiles to crawl across a new motorway being built in the south of France. It could make the difference between survival and extinction for the Hermann's tortoise, a rare breed that lives only in that region.

The planned route for the main road near the town of Toulon will cut in half the tortoises' favourite area, and might have played a part in wiping them out.

It will have an earthenware floor to make the tortoises feel comfortable, and shallow, sloping ends to make it easy for them to get in and out. When it's finished in two years, about 2,000 tortoises are expected to use the tunnel. That could make it almost as busy as the motorway.

Picture: Simon Walsh

2:2

Acid Rain

[Nearly forty] years ago, London experienced its worst peacetime disaster of the twentieth century. Four thousand people died, two thousand were hospitalised, and an uncounted number were distressingly ill. Animals choked to death, thousands of citizens were confined to their homes for a period of days, and transport in the capital came to an almost complete standstill.

The reason for this was a familiar and traditional one – smog. December 1952 was a cold month, and London's schools, hospitals, factories and homes were burning vast quantities of coal and oil. On the morning of 5 December, there was an atmospheric inversion – a layer of cold air squatted over the city, trapping the rising smoke, which concentrated in ever greater amounts at ground and rooftop level.

The result was a massive accumulation in the air of black dust and sulphur dioxide – a corrosive gas released when coal or oil is burnt – which blotted out the sun, made it impossible for people to see more than a yard in front of their faces, and destroyed the normal functionings of a capital city. 'The fog was so thick that you couldn't park your car', said one observer. 'Your passenger had to get out and stand at the kerb with a torch before you could even think about leaving the white line in the middle of the road.' People were injuring themselves so frequently by walking into the lamp posts in Whitehall that the authorities tied flares to the posts at eye-level... Eight seamen lost their ship, and asked a Port of London policeman to show them the way back to it; five minutes later, he fell into the Thames, closely followed by two of the sailors...

It was a particularly poisonous smog, containing sulphur fumes of a strength never before recorded in London. The effects on people's health were horrendous, and they died literally in their thousands – from respiratory diseases, disorders of the heart and circulatory system, and gastro-enteritis. The elderly, the very young, and those in poor health were particularly at risk.

What has all this to do with acid rain? There are two connections. Firstly, sulphur dioxide, a major contributor to the smog, is the central constituent of what is now called acid rain,

Reading for information

and it is produced in the air by the same processes which caused the London smogs. Secondly, the measures taken to alleviate London's smogs did not eradicate air pollution but merely transformed it. Instead of having short-term local effects, sulphur dioxide poisoning was transferred to a longer time-scale and began to affect a wider area.

After the 1952 smog, the government was faced with pressing calls for action and the result was the Clean Air Act 1956. Large areas of London were declared smokeless zones in which coal was forbidden for domestic use; factories and public utilities were ordered to clean the black dust from their smoke; and those industries which produced vast quantities of fumes – notably power stations – were instructed to build tall chimneys in order to carry exhaust gases away from the immediate vicinity.

The Clean Air Act was seen as immensely successful, and other countries followed the UK's lead ... There was one problem, however, which at the time went unnoticed but has since been given increasing importance: the production of sulphur dioxide continued, piped into the atmosphere by thousands of factories and industries throughout Europe. Millions of tonnes of this powerful pollutant are sent into the air every year. If the Clean Air Act had not been implemented and the London smogs had carried on, then public pressure would have forced the government to clean the sulphur dioxide, as well as the dust, out of industrial smoke.

Other European countries might then have joined the UK in restricting sulphur output, instead of piping the pollutant 400 feet into the air in the belief that it thus became harmless. If they had done this – and they did not – we would not now be witnessing the destruction of large parts of Europe's environment by acidic pollution. Acid rain is, the legacy of the London smogs.

This article is taken from an introduction to a book about acid rain. Other sources of information are magazines and other books.

▼ **Assignment 1**

Make a list of the difficult words and special terms used here. Look them up in a dictionary or ask your science teacher to explain them to you.

▼ **Assignment 2**

1 What is the passage about?
2 Why do you think the writer is angry about something that happened so long ago?
3 Did you find the passage interesting or not? Give reasons for your answer.

▼ **Assignment 3**

Design a clean air poster for NASP – the National Association for Smog Prevention. Use some written information to help get the seriousness of the problem across. Look at the advertisements at the beginning of the book and try to make your poster attract attention as these do.

▼ **Assignment 4**

You are going to write a scientific report about smog. Before you do that, look at the passage again and make notes about the following:
1 What caused smog?
2 How did the Clean Air Act stop smog?
3 What does the article think the Clean Air Act caused and how?

▼ **Assignment 5**

Writing a scientific report

Scientific reports are written in a different way to the article because they have different purposes and different readers.

The article describes smog and its effects in a way which tries to make you see the scene in London under the smog. To do this it uses a lot of adjectives (such as 'horrendous' and 'poisonous') and also tells little stories about the effect of the smog.

> **The carbon-oxygen cycle**
>
> Animals breathe in oxygen and breathe out carbon dioxide. Any animal trapped in an airtight place would soon die when all the available oxygen was used up. The Earth itself is like an airtight place surrounded by empty space – so what stops this happening on Earth...?

The purpose of a scientific report is to explain something as clearly and accurately as possible. It does not try to tell a colourful and attractive story. It is also often written for other scientists and so uses technical terms which they will understand without explanation. A scientific report would not need to explain the term 'inversion', but the article does.

Scientific reports also use headings to make it easy to see where information is, and often present their explanations or findings in diagrammatic forms, like the one below.

The **Smog Report Sheet** on the opposite page uses diagrams and headings to show the effects of smog and the Clean Air Act. Fill in the missing scientific information on a copy of the report sheet.

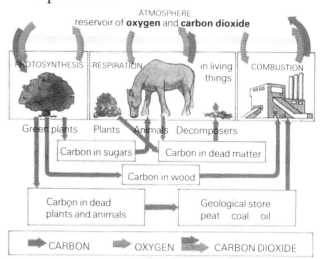

SMOG REPORT SHEET

Name: Date:

1. The 1952 London Smog was caused by _____

   The effects on the environment were _____

   The effects on people and animals were _____

2. The Clean Air Act was passed in _____

   The effect on smog was _____

   The effect on the environment was _____

   Acid rain is linked to smog because _____

3 ▶ FOCUS ON Following Instructions

Most people have to read instructions at some time – instructions on model kits, in recipe books, for getting somewhere. Here are some basic rules to follow:

- Read all the instructions through once quickly. At the same time try to think about what they are telling you to do.
- Think about the instructions for a minute.
- Now read them more carefully a second time.
- If you need any materials, assemble them carefully and prepare to follow the instructions step by step.

Following instructions

3:1

Using a Recipe

SPAGHETTI WITH BROCCOLI AND MUSHROOM SAUCE

Serves 4-6

5oz (125g) fresh mushrooms, sliced, or
1½ oz (40g) dried mushrooms
3 tablespoons oil
1 small onion, finely chopped
1 garlic clove, finely chopped
10oz (250g) broccoli
1 tin tomatoes, chopped
2 tablespoons tomato purée
1 vegetable stock cube
Fresh oregano or approximately 2 teaspoons dried oregano
1lb (400g) spaghetti
Chopped parsley, parmesan and a cup of cream (optional)

Sauté the onions in the oil with the garlic clove until the onions are just transparent. Add the mushrooms (soaked beforehand if you are using dried ones) and cook for five minutes, stirring all the time.

Heat a pan of boiling water and add the broccoli florets. Simmer for five minutes and drain. Keep broccoli to one side.

To the mushrooms add the tin of chopped tomatoes, vegetable stock cube, herbs, purée and water. Allow to simmer until sauce is a rich red colour. Add the broccoli and allow to simmer for a further 8-10 minutes.

Cook the spaghetti in boiling salted water until al dente.

To serve: Place the spaghetti on a serving dish and pour the sauce over the top. Swirl the cream (if you are using it) over the dish. Top with a sprinkling of parmesan and garnish with chopped parsley. Serve with a green salad.

Following instructions

▼ Assignment 1

Read the extract again. Then look at the following sentences. Which one matches most closely the way you read this passage?
- I read it all carefully and then understood by the end what it is I have to do.
- I read it quickly the first time, trying to picture in my mind the task I have to undertake. Then just to make sure I read it again more carefully.

When you read a recipe you are really reading a set of instructions. Think of the lessons in school where this happens. What types of lesson are they?

When we read instructions we normally read them through very quickly first, and then again to make sure we have understood them. You have to hold in your mind a picture of the whole process that you need to go through.

▼ Assignment 2

Now imagine that your friend wants to make the spaghetti and that you are going to instruct him or her. Make a list of instructions for them to follow without referring to your book.

▼ Assignment 3

1 Some of the words in this recipe come from other languages: sauté and al dente, for instance. You will find a lot of other words in recipes which come from other languages: roux, en croute, en papillote, escalope, julienne, mirepoix, panada, praline. See if you can find out what these words mean and where they come from.
2 Can you think of any reasons why these words have come into English from other languages? (Think of where dishes like spaghetti come from.)

3:2

Making a Papier Mâché Model

▼ Assignment 1

On the next page there are instructions for making the papier mâché models shown opposite. Unfortunately the editor has made a mistake and has placed the diagrams which go with the instructions in the wrong order. Read the instructions carefully, and then decide which order the diagrams should go in.

▼ Assignment 2

The writer of the page in this craft book has to contact the editor to tell him or her about the mistake. As the book is being printed that day, she has to ring the editor up and explain the error, and how it can be corrected, over the phone. Choose one person from each group. Sit back to back and with a copy of the diagrams in front of you. Decide who will be the writer and who will be the editor and act out the conversation that could take place in this situation.

▼ Assignment 3

Imagine that you are going to make some puppets in your English class to use in a play you have written. Your teacher has agreed to this. However, he or she is worried about the mess that could be made and has asked you to write some instructions explaining to the whole class the following:
- materials needed and where they can be obtained
- storage of materials and puppets
- where water can be obtained for making the puppets
- procedures for clearing up at the end of each lesson

Following instructions

Arm puppets

You will need:

Several old newspapers – about 32 large double sheets for pulping, and more besides (see below); 3 pints (1.7 litre) cold water; 4 level tablespoons cellulose wallpaper adhesive (Polycell); thick stick; clear varnish; coloured stretch-nylon sock; old cup; small varnish or paint brush; turpentine substitute to clean brush; wool; household glue; lace doilies; large bucket; paints; adhesive tape.

To make the puppets:

1

Tear up the 32 sheets of newspaper into very small pieces and put into the bucket. Pour very hot water over them, taking care not to splash yourself. Leave to soak about 36 hours, stirring occasionally, and pounding with the stick.

2

Remove the soaked paper, squeezing out as much water as possible (as this is a messy job, it is advisable to wear rubber gloves). Clean bucket.

3

Pour the cold water into the empty bucket, add the cellulose wallpaper adhesive, stir well and leave to stand for 15 minutes.

4

Put about 3–4 tablespoons of the mixture into an old cup. Leave on one side. Break the soaked newspaper into the paste mixture in the bucket, and stir and pound until all the adhesive is absorbed.

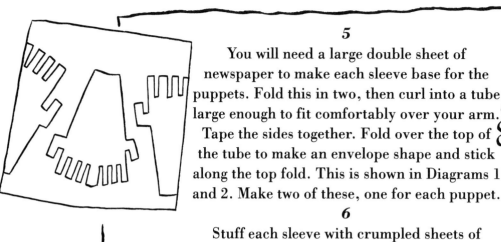

5

You will need a large double sheet of newspaper to make each sleeve base for the puppets. Fold this in two, then curl into a tube large enough to fit comfortably over your arm. Tape the sides together. Fold over the top of the tube to make an envelope shape and stick along the top fold. This is shown in Diagrams 1 and 2. Make two of these, one for each puppet.

6

Stuff each sleeve with crumpled sheets of newspaper until it is full and firm. Take a handful of the papier mâché and press it round the sleeve (Diagram 3). Continue until the shape is covered with pulp. Build up more around the ears, and an exaggeratedly large amount for Punch's nose and chin… Leave in a warm place until quite dry.

7

Thoroughly paste one side of half a large sheet of newspaper, using the reserved mixture in the cup. Fold in half, paste the top of the paper and fold again. Then paste and fold once more. Smooth the top firmly to remove any air bubbles, then leave to dry.

8

Cut two pairs of arms and hands from the pasted, folded newspaper. Follow the shapes shown in Diagram 4.

Finishing:

Paint the faces, bodies, arms and hands of the puppets, leave to dry and then varnish. If your paint is quickly absorbed, you might like to apply a second coat, so that you get a good strong colour, before varnishing.

9

Clean the varnish brush in turpentine substitute, then wash in soap and cold water.

10

The hair of both puppets is made with thick wool-rug wool is best, but double-knitting wool or quick-knitting wool would do. Arrange this over the heads in untidy strands and glue into place.

11

Judy's little dust-cap is cut from a lace doily. Glue this in place, pinching it up at the centre. Follow Diagram 5 for position.

12

No Punch puppet is complete without a large, stiff ruff at the neck. This one is made from three doilies. Cut out a hole in the middle, then pinch and pleat to make the collar stand out well. Alternatively, soak the doilies in the glue mixture after forming the ruff. Leave to dry and then glue around the puppet's neck (Diagram 6).

13

His hat is made from the toe of a coloured sock. Cut off just below the heel, turn cut end inwards to hide the rough edge, then pull on to the puppet's head. Glue in place.

14

The puppets are now ready to play. Don't forget that Punch is often is often aggressive , and that Judy usually gives as good as she gets!

3:3

Craft Design

▼ Assignment 1

Study the diagrams for making this paper plane carefully. This time the instructions have been jumbled up and need to be rewritten. Can you place them in the order that they should be written in?

▼ Assignment 2

Following your instructions, try to make the paper plane.

▼ Assignment 3

Write similar detailed instructions to someone on how to boil an egg or make a cup of tea. Draw accompanying diagrams if you can.

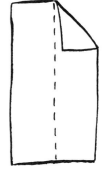

The paper dart

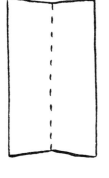

Gently throw the dart across the room aiming it slightly upwards.

Repeat this with edges 's' and 't'.

Straighten the wings out so that they are parallel with the floor.

Does it fly straight or curve to one side?

Turn the dart over and do the same to the other side

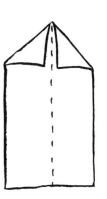

Following instructions

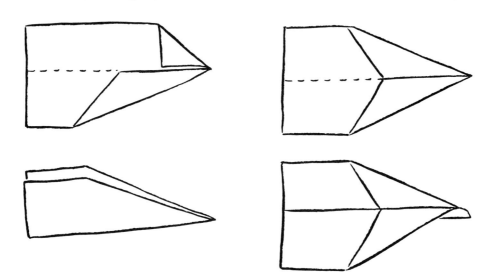

Take a sheet of A4 paper. Fold it down the middle of its length then open it out.

Fold the wing down about 1–1.5 cm from the centre fold.

Bend the points into the body of the dart (5–8 mm).

Fold the dart so that the folded parts are on the inside.

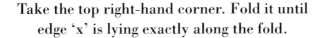

Take the top right-hand corner. Fold it until edge 'x' is lying exactly along the fold.

Take the top left-hand corner. Fold it until edge 'y' is lying exactly along the fold.

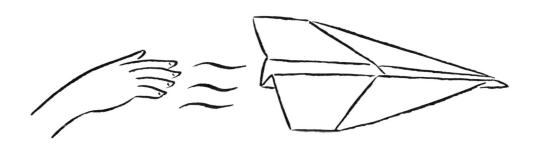

4 FOCUS ON Reference Skills

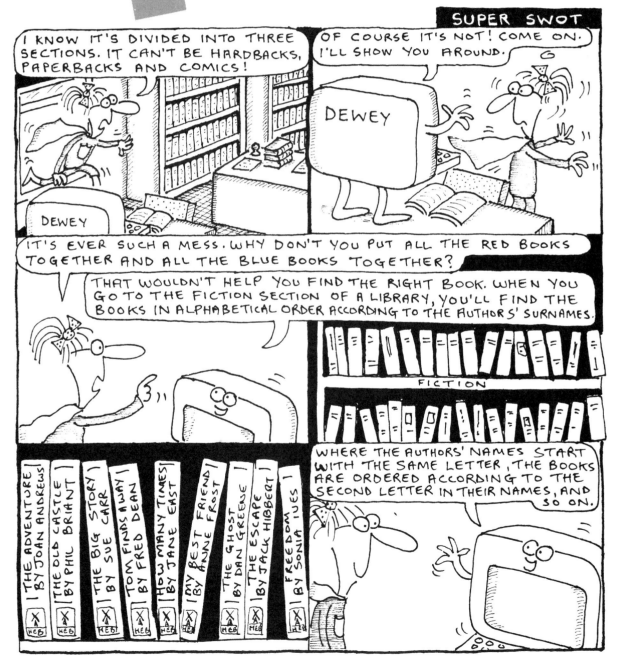

Reference skills

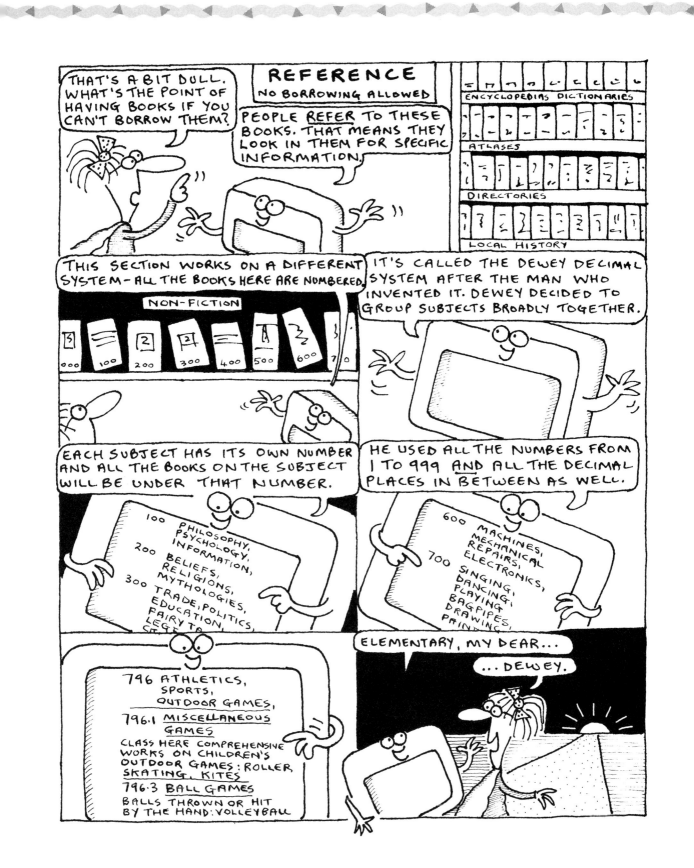

4:1

Using a Book

```
Z T S E S A L T A Y U M F D S
W K R Q I H N F S X I Y I I T
T S D W J A O V A N T L E C N
O T I T L E N L I S O L U T E
Y X G A S Y F K D F R A K I T
R J J U Y T I X E K E C D O N
I S G T X D C R P T F I F N O
E D D H M Y T L O J E T Z A C
D F I O B E I J L Z R E Y R G
J G K R T A O S C T E B K Y B
S P I N E G N D Y V N A N P X
N U H J Y J T G C M C H M R E
R N O I T C I F N W E P G E D
L Z D V H S H M E B S L X H N
K W E J D E W E Y M Z A Q H I
```

▼ **Assignment 1**

Match the following definitions with their words. Then find the words in the word search. They are there horizontally or vertically, backwards or forwards. Most of the answers can be found in the pages before this or on the opposite page, but some you should know already.

Definitions
- The name of a book is its.....
- A table listing what a book contains.
- An..... is found at the back of a book.
- Books giving information on all branches of knowledge.
- Section of books that can only be used in the library.
- Name given to the section of books that are based on fact.
- A book listing words and their meanings.
- An invented story.
- A person who writes books is called an.....
- A book of maps.
- The system of numbers used to categorise reference books is called this.
- This part of the body is the backbone of any book.
- Most fiction is arranged this way.

4:2

Finding your Way Around a Book

The contents list is found at the beginning of the book and tells you what you will find inside.

The index is found at the back of the book and is arranged alphabetically.

The running heads divide nonfiction works up in the way that chapters divide fiction. In nonfiction, the running heads make it easy for readers to find quickly the section of the work that they want to read.

This is the ISBN number – a unique identifying number given to each book on publication. Knowing the title and author as well as this special number can make ordering a book in a library much easier. Can you find the ISBN number for *this* book?

CONTENTS

PART ONE WEIMAR GERMANY, 1918–33

1.1 The Beginning of the Weimar Republic, 1918–19
1.2 The Treaty of Versailles

INDEX

Anschluss (1938) 49
Anti-Comintern Pact (1936) 48
appeasement 50, 51
army 23, 26, 27, 36, 37
Article 48 (Republic Constitution) 5
Auschwitz 35, 47, 58, 59

Munich *Putsch* (1923) 8, 12,
imprisonment 15
refounds party 15
ideas 16, 17, 18
Depression and rise to power
how people saw him 20, 21

PART ONE WEIMAR GERMANY, 1918–33

1.2 THE TREATY OF VERSAILLES

ISBN 0-340-53462-1

4:3 Using a Dictionary

A dictionary has a special type of page layout to help you find the information you need.

Running heads help you find the page your word is on. So, if you're looking for *scarf*, you know it falls between *scap*... and *scat*... so it must be on this page.

Headwords - these are the words you are looking for.

Parts of speech - this tells you whether the word is a noun, verb, adverb etc.

Specialist term - if the word is used in a certain subject or field, this is shown here.

---

scapula   922   scatter diagram

scapula (*say* skap-yoo-la) *noun* also called a **shoulder-blade**
Anatomy: either of two large triangular bones behind the shoulder.
Word Family: **scapular**, *adjective*.
[Latin]

scar (1) *noun*
a mark left by a healed cut or wound, e.g. on the human skin or on a plant where a leaf was once attached.
Usage: 'your gossip left a *scar* on my reputation' (= blemish).
scar *verb*
(**scarred, scarring**)
to mark with a scar or scars: 'the bombs *scarred* the countryside with giant craters'.
[Greek *eskhara* a scab]

scar (2) *noun*
a steep rocky place or cliff.

scarab (*say* skarrab) *noun*
a) a type of beetle considered sacred by the ancient Egyptians. b) an image or carving in the shape of a scarab.
[from Greek]

scarce (*say* skairce) *adjective*
in short supply: 'tomatoes were *scarce* during the floods'.
make oneself scarce, to leave or keep out of the way.
scarcely *adverb*
barely or hardly: 'there were *scarcely* 25 people at the meeting'.
scarcity (*say* skairsi-tee) *noun*
shortness of supply: 'the *scarcity* of tomatoes was caused by the floods'.
Word Family: **scarceness**, *noun*, **scarcity**.
[Latin *excerptus* picked out]

scare (*rhymes with* air) *verb*
to frighten.
scare *noun*
a feeling of fear or alarm: a) 'you gave me quite a *scare*'; b) 'after the cyclone there was a *scare* of cholera'.

scarecrow *noun*
1. an object, usually a figure of a man in old clothes, set up to scare birds away from a crop.
2. a) a person or thing with a ragged or frightening appearance. b) a very thin person.

scarf (1) *noun*
plural is **scarves**
a strip or square of cloth worn around the head or neck.
Word Family: **scarf**, *verb*.

scarf (2) *noun*
plural is **scarfs**
a joint made by fitting two tapered pieces together.

scarify (*say* skairi-fie) *verb*
(**scarified, scarifying**)
1. to scratch or break the surface of.
2. to criticize severely.
Word Family: **scarification**, *noun*.

scarlet *noun*
a vivid reddish-orange colour.
Word Family: **scarlet**, *adjective*.

scarlet fever
also called **scarlatina**
an infectious bacterial disease causing tonsillitis and a red rash.

scarlet runner
see RUNNER BEAN.

scarp *noun*
a steep slope or ridge of rock.
[from Italian]

scarper *verb*
(*informal*) to run away, especially after having done something wrong.
[rhyming slang *Scapa Flow* = go]

scary (*say* skairi) *adjective*
(*informal*) frightening.

scat *interjection*
(*informal*) go away!
[for SCATTER]

scathing (*say* skay-*thing*) *adjective*
severely critical or scornful: 'a *scathing* review of a bad film'.
Word Family: **scathingly**, *adverb*.

scatology (*say* ska-tolla-jee) *noun*
the continual use in literature of images of human waste, etc.
Word Family: **scatological**, *adjective*.
[Greek *skatos* of dung + -LOGY]

scatter *verb*
to send, move or distribute in many different directions: a) 'we *scattered* the seed on the ploughed land'; b) 'the crowd *scattered* when it heard the sirens'.
Word Family: **scattering**, *noun*, a scattered number or quantity.

scatterbrain *noun*
a person who cannot remember or concentrate on things.
Word Family: **scatterbrained**, *adjective*.

scatter diagram
Maths: a graph which compares two variables, such as the health and wealth of a population. The distribution of the resultant coordinate points shows the degree of correlation between the variables.

Word family - words are often like other words which have similar meanings. This grouping is called a word family.

Pronunciation - how to say the headword.

Derivation - many words in English come from other languages, and their origin can be found in a dictionary.

Definition - the meaning of the word. If it has more than one, the meanings are listed and often numbered.

Reference skills

▼ Assignment 1

Look at the following list of words that have been adopted into the language recently. Find out from a dictionary what they mean. Can you work out why they've come into the language recently and where they come from?

▼ Assignment 2

Choose at least ten of these words and write a piece about your school and area, including these words as the boy who wrote the extract has done.

iceberg lettuce
sarnies
listeriosis
minneola

star fruit
mega
one-stop
plonkers

condos
laptops
mountain bikes
high tech

world music
icing
sexy

Take a leaf out of our book

MY right honourable colleagues. There is a desperate problem in the world today. Industry always comes first and the environment second. What must we do to change this?

We don't want our rainforests to just walk. If we in the pole position all got together we could tackle this problem with the crispness of an **iceberg lettuce**.

First we need to check out how much rainforest is left. From rainforests we get remedies for cancer and fruit for fruit bowls.

Who wants to eat empty **sarnies** for the rest of their life for fear of **listeriosis**. We want exotic fruits like **minneola** and

Liam Blake, 10, from Surrey

star fruit which only grow in tropical areas.

Think of what we are in danger of losing! You may think Kew Gardens is **mega** but that is nothing compared to what you would see in a rainforest for its **one-stop** and beautiful at the same time.

So away with the **plonkers** who live in their flashy little **condos** and ride around with their neat little **laptops**. They don't care about the environment.

Let us take a leaf (green of course) from our right honourable colleague Norman Tebbit.

We must get on our **mountain bikes** and ride through the rainforest to see their wonders and to meet their people whose lifestyle may not be **high tech** but whose food is real! Let our music be **world music**!!

So no more fighting over **icing** on the world cake. The task is now to make saving our environment **sexy**.

FOCUS ON Selecting Information

Scanning is a term given to what we do when we are looking for particular information in amongst a lot of other material.

Can you think of times when this happens? Look at the pictures below:

Scanning involves looking quickly over all the material until you find the information that interests you. Then you can read this information carefully and thoroughly. Try doing this in the following assignment.

The Speed Game

You need a copy of the Alton Towers map on pages 46 and 47 in front of you.

1 Put a circle around all the signs for toilets.
2 Put a triangle around the information centres.
3 Put a star beside all the places where you can find something to eat.
4 Underline the following:
   Dragon Rollercoaster
   Chinese Temple
   Skyride Station
   Spider
   Miniature Railway
   Doll's Exhibition
5 List the rides with height restrictions.
6 How many new rides are there?
7 You are going to Alton Towers with your grandmother and with your eight-year-old sister. Your grandmother likes gardens and exhibitions. Your sister likes rides but is afraid of very high ones. Choose four things your grandmother might like and four things your sister might like. Then choose the four things you would like to do most.

In what order would you visit all twelve places? Remember, you don't want to walk too far and you will need to eat at some point. Plan your time at Alton Towers and draw a line on the map to show which way you will go round.

KEY

- ○ FAMILY RIDES/ATTRACTIONS
- ○ CHILDRENS RIDES
- ○ WHITE KNUCKLE RIDES
- ● FAST FOOD/SNACKS
- ○ SEATED RESTAURANTS
- ● SHOPS

* Height restriction applies on this ride
† Height restriction applies on this ride unless accompanied by an adult
Inclement weather or mechanical difficulties may cause delays or cancellations.

- ⓘ INFORMATION CENTRE
  - Wheelchairs
  - Pushchairs
  - Lockers
- 🚻 TOILETS
- ♿ TOILETS FOR DISABLED
- ⓘ INFORMATION BOOTHS
- ✚ MEDICAL CENTRE
  - FIRST AID
  - LOST CHILDREN
  - BABY FEEDING FACILITIES
- £ BUREAU DE CHANGE
- S SECURITY
- ☎ TELEPHONES

FESTIVAL PARK
Alton Towers

- 1001 NIGHTS
- CORKSCREW
- DRAGON ROLLERCOASTER
- ENTERPRISE
- WAVESWINGER
- SPIDER
- FESTIVAL PARK ARCADE
- DUTCH FRIES KITCHEN
- TASTE OF THE ORIENT

THE TOWERS
Alton Towers

THE GARDENS
Alton Towers

- THUNDER LOOPER
- SKYRIDE STATION
- THUNDER LOOPER SNACKS
- PAGODA FOUNTAIN
- BANDSTAND
- CONSERVATORIES
- CHINESE TEMPLE
- MINIATURE RAILWAY
- CORKSCREW FOUNTAIN
- SWISS COTTAGE RESTAURANT
- MONORAIL (FROM CAR PARK)
- MISSISSIPPI SHOW BOAT
- TASTE OF AMERICA
- FLUME BURGER
- FLUME DOUGHNUT
- FLUME FRIES
- PIZZA POTATO FOOD COURT

46

The map on these pages may be photocopied for classroom use.

5:1

Planning a Holiday

In this section you are going to put your scanning skills to good use in planning a holiday for the Gale family in Weymouth. First study carefully the information that you are given about the family.

John Gale, age 45

Power station worker (ex-navy).

Likes photographing castles, forts and architecture and watching comedy shows on television. Enjoys all sport, especially watching rugby league and swimming. Favourite pastimes include bird watching and sea-fishing. Likes looking around museums and hates shopping.

Member of Hull Ornithologists' Society, the RSPB and Acton Gardening Club.

Favourite food: Fish and chips.

Ambitions: To see Corfe Castle.

Mary Gale, age 42

Auxiliary nurse in local cottage hospital.

Likes reading, knitting, horse-riding and playing golf. Enjoys running and swimming and completed the London Marathon. Also enjoys shopping for clothes and browsing round craft shops. Hates looking around museums.

Member of Acton Writers' Circle and Timberley Amateur Dramatic Group.

Favourite food: All Chinese food.

Ambitions: To see Hardy's birthplace, and to run a marathon in under 4 hours.

Susan Gale, age 13

Likes watching *Top of the Pops* and *Neighbours*, and painting. Enjoys horse-riding, buying clothes and tourist attractions.

Member of Acton Pony Club, Timberley Swimming Club, the RSPB and Model Railway Club.

Favourite food: Chips and vegetarian food.

Ambitions: To open a shop that sells paintings and craftware. (Susan won a first prize in a major national art competition this year.)

Special information: Susan has to complete a special summer homework assignment. She has decided to undertake a project on dinosaurs. This is a cross-curricular piece of work involving producing work for the English and Art departments as well as Humanities.

Simon Gale, age 15

Likes travelling on trains, fishing, horse-riding and watching cowboy films. Is a heavy metal fan and enjoys visiting record shops. Has a collection of over two hundred albums by various groups. Is a DJ at the local hospital radio station and wants to do this for a living. Also enjoys playing squash, fishing, visiting forts and anything to do with the military, especially tanks. Has just completed a diving course.

Member of the RSPB and the local Angling Society as well as Greenpeace.

Favourite food: American-style beefburgers and chilli.

Ambitions: To be rich and famous, and to take Madonna out for a meal and impress her!

Special information: For one of his English GCSE assignments Simon has to write about places he has visited in the summer. He would like to write something about the tank museum, the fort and the maritime centre.

Jessica Gale, age 64

Retired school bus-driver, has a public service vehicle licence.

Likes knitting, her grandchildren and spending money on clothes. Hobbies include fishing, horse-riding and helping out in the local museum. She also presses wild flowers and makes greetings cards and pictures to sell.

Member of Timberley Bowls Club, the County Bowling Team and the local history society.

Favourite food: Roast beef and Yorkshire pudding with horseradish sauce.

Ambitions: To get into the English bowling team and visit Jersey or Guernsey

Selecting information

The family will be based just outside Weymouth but wish to travel extensively around the area, as they have never been to this part of Dorset before. John and Mary chose this area because the whole family will be able to do or see something that they would like. They also realised that the family have different tastes in food and each of them will have a chance to choose the restaurant or café that the family will eat in that day.

One day just before the holiday the family looked at all the information on the following pages and planned a list of visits that the family could make. They only planned out seven full days and allowed the other seven to be rest days, when the family could lounge around the campsite or just go into the local town. They thought that otherwise they would all get tired of rushing around as a family. The three adults all drive and they have brought the family car with them.

▼ **Assignment 1**

Write down the name of each character across a page, and under each make a list of the types of activity that he or she might wish to do on this holiday.

▼ **Assignment 2**

Scan through all the information that follows. Then, under the list you made above, add the names of places that each person would find interesting to visit.

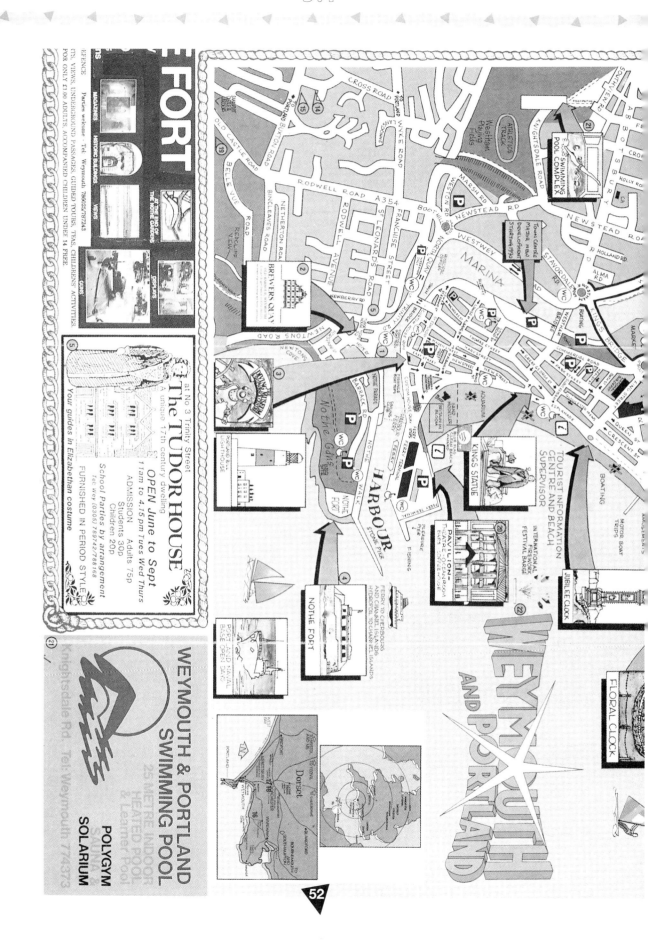

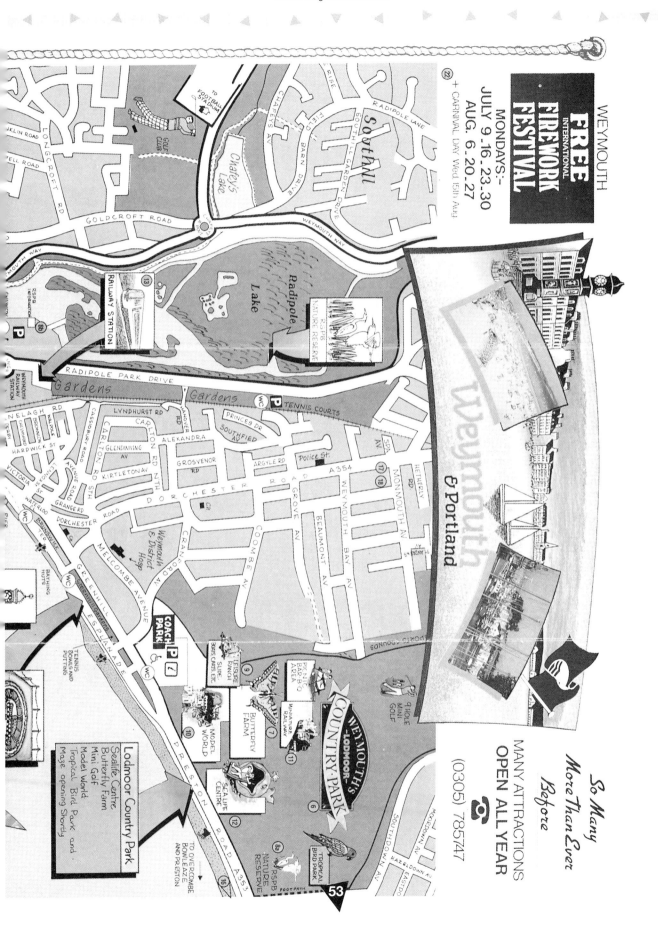

▼ Assignment 3

On a large piece of paper try to plan seven days' activities for the family that will ensure they all get to see or do things they would like. You might decide that on some days some of the family would not want to visit all the places, but would go off by themselves and all meet later. However, for most of the time the family should be together on these days. Make sure that they all get the chance to choose where they will eat as a family, so that they can all get to eat their favourite food at least once.

▼ Assignment 4

Write the postcards which Susan or Simon might have written home to friends, giving details of the holiday that you are having.

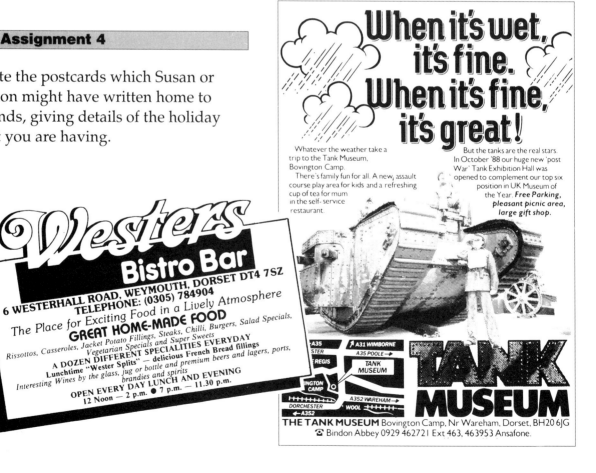

SEA CHEF RESTAURANT & TAKEAWAY

FOR THE VERY BEST FISH AND CHIPS

Wide range of takeaway food also available or come and sit down in our cosy restaurant for a slap up fish and chip meal. Children's menu available.

Open 10.30 a.m. to 10.30 p.m.
7 days a week

You will find us at:
2 KINGS STREET
next to Weymouth's famous Joke Shop

LOCAL SEAFOODS A SPECIALITY

*Morning Coffee from 9.30 a.m.
Light Lunches
Full a la Carte Menu including Local Fish Dishes.
Fresh Meat Specialities and an extensive range of Vegetarian Dishes*
Lunch from 12 Noon
Dinner from 6.30 pm

Milton Arms
17th Century
Licensed Restaurant and Gallery Gift Shop

**21 ST. ALBAN STREET
WEYMOUTH
TEL: WEYMOUTH 782767
OR 787887**

NORMAN & DAPHNE HANNEY

The Deep Sea Adventure

Live diving displays

★ Three floors of animated and interactive displays
★ Children's play submarine, computer games
★ Disabled facilities, lift to all floors, souvenir shop

TITANIC THE UNSINKABLE LEGEND

Special for '89

The Diving Museum & Shipwreck Centre
The Old Harbour, Weymouth. Tel 760690

SANG LEE
CHINESE RESTAURANT
FULLY LICENCED
**59 PARK STREET, WEYMOUTH
TELEPHONE: 776050**

Opening Times: Mon-Sat 12 noon-2 p.m.
5 p.m.-11 p.m. Open Sunday 5 p.m.-11 p.m.
Business Lunches from Mon to Fri
12 noon-2 p.m.

Po Sun
Chinese Food to Take Away
**61 PARK STREET, WEYMOUTH
TELEPHONE 783327**
Telephone Orders Welcome

Opening Times: Mon-Sat 12 noon-2 p.m.
5 p.m.-Midnight, Sunday 5 p.m.-Midnight

NEAR THE RAILWAY STATION

5:1

EXCURSIONS TO JERSEY & GUERNSEY FROM WEYMOUTH

GUERNSEY NIGHTFLIER MONDAY & WEDNESDAY	SUNDAY EXCURSIONS TO JERSEY
DEP(W) 23.30 ARR(G) 06.30	DEP(W) 08.00 ARR(J) 18.00
DEP(G) 13.30 ARR(W) 19.00	DEP(J) 22.00 ARR(W) 06.00
7 HOURS ASHORE	**3 HOURS ASHORE**
PLUS OPTIONAL ISLAND COACH TOUR WITH FULL ENGLISH BREAKFAST ONLY **£5.50**	BOTH ONLY **£15.00** ADULT **£8.00** CHILD

SEE THE SIGHTS, GET YOUR DUTY FREE ALLOWANCE
NO PASSPORT REQUIRED

WMS WEYMOUTH MARITIME SERVICES
0305 788300

WEYMOUTH BUTTERFLY FARM & JUNGLE SAFARI

This farm in the middle of Lodmoor Country Park — Weymouth's fastest expanding leisure area with a Sealife Centre, amusements, mini-golf, bar-B-Q and picnic areas, Shire Horse Centre and extensive nature reserve. Lodmoor is on the outskirts of town but within yards of the famous beach. Main car and coach park. The farm enjoys a large jungle flight area, caterpillar breeding centre, education and video facilities and, among many others in the insect house, Boris, TV's favourite tarantula.

FULL COLOUR POSTER inside

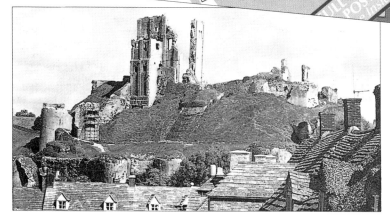

Selecting information

▼ Assignment 5

As part of her dinosaur project, Susan has to keep a diary and write down details of any information she finds, explain where she got her information and draw a map of any specific places visited. Write her diary account of a visit that she might have made. This work, including diagrams, should cover at least two sides.

Britains only Dinosaur Museum

Unique—exciting—amazing
All weather attraction

THE DINOSAUR MUSEUM
DORCHESTER

Corner of Durngate Street and Icen Way
TELEPHONE DORCHESTER (0305) 69880

OPEN EVERY DAY

The DINOSAUR MUSEUM is like no other museum in Britain - it's unique. Actual fossils, skeletons and lifesize reconstructions combine with audio-visual and interactive displays to inform and entertain.

The fascinating world of dinosaurs is brought to life in a new and exciting way.

Exciting additions to the museum for this year are two new life-size reconstructions of dinosaurs - Triceratops and Corythosaurus; a new exhibition gallery depicting the Prehistoric World after the dinosaurs; plus many new fossils, some seen for the first time in Britain, linked to new displays.

The Dinosaur Museum is now more than ever a fun visit for all the family and Dorset's Monster Attraction. It is situated in Icen Way, Dorchester and is open every day from 9.30 a.m. to 5.30 p.m.

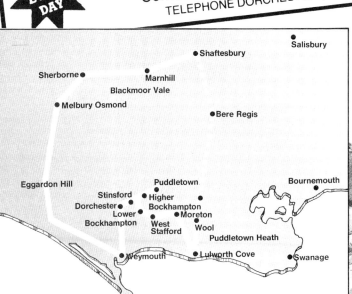

5:2

Designing a Tourist Brochure

▼ **Assignment 1**

The local Tourist Information Office have also asked Susan and Simon to take part in a competition to design a tourist brochure specifically for young people. Design the brochure that they might have designed and written. Remember that this will need illustrating. It has to include details about what is available in Weymouth and the surrounding area – the extent of this area is left for you to decide.

▼ **Assignment 2**

Pictures can be very important in advertising and giving information, and they are used in tourist brochures to attract people to a resort. Each of the pictures opposite builds up an idea in a viewer's mind as to what Weymouth is like. Susan and Simon want to use two of the pictures in their brochure, but they can't agree which two. As a group, decide which you would use and explain what impression a reader might get of Weymouth from those pictures, and from the ones you left out.

Selecting information

6 FOCUS ON Reading Pictures

How good are you at reading pictures?

Pictures, like words, have a message to convey, and it's often important to understand what they are saying. You can read them in much the same way as words, either in great detail to see exactly what's happening in them or by scanning quickly for a general impression.

To start off, look at the two pictures below very carefully and see if you can spot twenty differences between them.

When you have finished your list of differences, sit back to back with a partner and take turns to describe them to each other.

Reading pictures

▼ Assignment 1

Before you read any of the words in the cartoon, look carefully at the pictures and say what atmosphere they conjure up. What sort of action would you expect to happen here?

Now read the plot so far and tackle assignment 2.

The plot so far:

Macbeth is Thane of Glamis (a thane is a title similar to that of lord today). He has helped his king, Duncan, to win a bloody battle and is coming back across a lonely moor to meet him. He is met by three witches, who greet him with the words, 'All hail Macbeth! that shalt be king hereafter.' They also call him Thane of Cawdor, a title that Duncan gives him shortly afterwards as a reward for his part in the battle. He is unnerved by the witches, especially when their prophecy that he will be Thane of Cawdor immediately comes true. He writes a letter to his wife telling her of the strange events and about the prophecy.

▼ Assignment 2

Read the following rough modernised version of Lady Macbeth's thoughts:

You are already Thane of Glamis and Cawdor and shall be what is promised to you. But I fear that you have not the nature for it. You are too kind to think of taking the quickest route. You have the ambition but not the wickedness needed to carry out the deed. You want to achieve your ambition by playing fair. Though you would not do anything bad yourself, you would accept the gains from a bad deed. You want to be king, but you must commit murder to get the crown. It's more that you are afraid of committing the murder than that you don't want the murder done. Hurry here to me.

As a group, decide what you learn about Lady Macbeth and Macbeth from her words. She obviously has a plan she wants to tell Macbeth. What do you think it might be?

6:1

ACT I Scene VII

IF IT WERE DONE, WHEN 'TIS DONE, THEN 'TWERE WELL IT WERE DONE QUICKLY. IF TH'ASSASSINATION COULD TRAMMEL UP THE CONSEQUENCE, AND CATCH WITH HIS SURCEASE, SUCESS; THAT BUT THIS BLOW MIGHT BE THE BE-ALL AND THE END-ALL — HERE,

BUT HERE, UPON THIS BANK AND SHOAL OF TIME, WE'D JUMP THE LIFE TO COME. BUT IN THESE CASES WE STILL HAVE JUDGEMENT HERE, THAT WE BUT TEACH BLOODY INSTRUCTIONS, WHICH BEING TAUGHT RETURN TO PLAGUE TH'INVENTOR. THIS EVEN-HANDED JUSTICE COMMENDS TH'INGREDIENCE OF OUR POISONED CHALICE TO OUR OWN LIPS. HE'S HERE IN DOUBLE TRUST:

FIRST, AS I AM HIS KINSMAN AND HIS SUBJECT, STRONG BOTH AGAINST THE DEED; THEN, AS HIS HOST, WHO SHOULD AGAINST HIS MURDERER SHUT THE DOOR, NOT BEAR THE KNIFE MYSELF. BESIDES, THIS DUNCAN HATH BORNE HIS FACULTIES SO MEEK, HATH BEEN SO CLEAR IN HIS GREAT OFFICE, THAT HIS VIRTUES WILL PLEAD LIKE ANGELS, TRUMPET-TONGUED AGAINST THE DEEP DAMNATION OF HIS TAKING-OFF.

AND PITY, LIKE A NAKED NEW-BORN BABE, STRIDING THE BLAST, OR HEAVEN'S CHERUBIN, HORSED UPON THE SIGHTLESS COURIERS OF THE AIR, SHALL BLOW THE HORRID DEED IN EVERY EYE, THAT TEARS SHALL DROWN THE WIND. I HAVE NO SPUR TO PRICK THE SIDES OF MY INTENT, BUT ONLY VAULTING AMBITION, WHICH O'ERLEAPS ITSELF, AND FALLS ON TH'OTHER —

Reading pictures

▼ **Assignment 1**

In this scene, Duncan is visiting Macbeth and Lady Macbeth. Lady Macbeth wants to kill the king. What does Macbeth feel about it? Again, before you read the words in the cartoon, work out from the pictures what you think Macbeth is thinking and feeling.

▼ **Assignment 2**

Read the rough modernised version of the extract on the right.

List the reasons that Macbeth gives for not committing the murder. Do you think the pictures give a true impression of what he is thinking and feeling? Do you think he will kill Duncan? Why, or why not?

▼ **Assignment 3**

Try reading Macbeth's words aloud in your groups, matching the way you sound to what he is saying. Take turns to read the parts of his thoughts in the different frames of the cartoon.

> If murder were over and done with once it's done, then it would be best to do it quickly. If the killing could block off everything that follows from it, and his death could guarantee success – if this blow could end it all here, in this life on earth – we'd take the risk of being judged in the afterlife. But in these cases we are still judged here; in killing Duncan in such a manner, I would be teaching another to do the same to me. He trusts me as a kinsman and as a subject, and both are strong reasons for not killing him. But more than this, I am his host. I should shut the door against the murderer, not bear the knife myself. Besides, Duncan has used his authority as king in such a modest fashion, and has been so free from corruption, that his good qualities will plead like angels against the evil deed if he is murdered. Tears of pity at the horror of the deed will fall from so many eyes that the wind itself will be drowned. It is only ambition that spurs me on this path.

7 FOCUS ON Drama

Greg Cullen talks to us about why stories and drama mean so much to us.

Why are stories so important to human beings? We all know many stories, such as *Cinderella*. Stories take up a huge part of our lives – for example, we listen to the Bible or to the Koran, read novels and comics, tell jokes, discuss the lives of characters in soap operas ('I think she should tell him that the baby is not his'), watch films and videos. Another type of story is created when we play or take part in a drama lesson. When small children play mummies and daddies they are rehearsing for life, coming to understand the behaviour they see around them. They learn what it is to be alive and human.

It is not because the stories are 'true' in the sense that we can say that they actually happened. Stories are made up and are often not logical. Red Riding Hood would have to have been blind or had an extremely hairy granny not to notice that it was a wolf in her bed. Stories are stupid, aren't they? Yet we, in our technological world, still love to hear of Merlin the magician.

Why do we give up our daily hold on reality and instead enjoy nonsense? Or is it really as nonsensical as all that? Human beings have powers no other animal has. We have a complex language which can be recorded for all time. We are able to feel what it must be like to be in someone else's shoes. In a story we can know more about a situation than any of its characters, which we cannot do in our own lives. When a murderer is on the loose in somebody's house, we sit on the edge of our seats when an innocent person goes to investigate. We can understand a character's feelings or respond to an imaginary situation. Think for a moment of how you imagine scenes where you can tell a person what you really think of them. We can all create stories.

In order for us to feel emotions in a drama we must understand what the character wants and who or what is stopping them from getting it; Macbeth wants to be king but Duncan is on the throne. The barrier to success may, however, also lie within a character, and in the right situation a flaw such as greed or vanity might prove fatal. As an audience we can condemn Macbeth's actions but also understand the human failing we share with him. We can judge. The theatre has throughout history been a forum for debating what's right. 'Should she tell him the baby is his or not?' – even soap opera debates the rights and wrongs of a situation and let us practise deciding how we should behave and what we believe in.

Stories are not necessarily real but they can teach us more about what the world is like than the news can.

Stories also work on us in another way. To conquer the ugly sisters and stepmother makes Cinderella feel worthwhile. The slipper fits, she is special after all. We all feel sometimes that no one appreciates us, that others get a better deal and are more loved than we are. When we see *Cinderella* in the theatre we do not necessarily say or think, 'Oh, yes, I felt as Cinderella does,' but we unconsciously recognise

the way she feels. We are glad when Cinderella becomes more wealthy, more truly loved than her sisters and overcomes those who want to stop her getting what she wants. Why? Because we all wish we could do that. Stories can give us comfort in a world which can be hurtful. At a deep, unconscious level they fulfil our wishes.

The theatre has remained hugely popular because it has one special quality – it is about human beings and it is live. Because of this, performances in the theatre use everything which makes us human. Good actors draw from their imagination, intuition, emotions, intellect, physical and spiritual being and from their own experience and interpretations of life, just as a child does in play. In the world of stories a wolf may take the place of your granny and witches can foresee your future, but they will only be 'true' to us if the actors use their whole selves to make us feel familiar feelings. We laugh, cry, feel angry or reassured when we understand or recognise. The theatre entertains us because we can play again, pretend it's real; we too can rehearse for life and reflect upon what it is really like to be alive and human.

7:1 Pantomime

Pantomime is a very old form of drama, which has been traced back to ancient Rome. It has its own strong traditions. It usually has a main male character who is played by a woman, and a chief comedian who is a man dressed up as a woman – the 'pantomime dame'.

The dialogue in pantomime always moves along very quickly with lots of corny jokes, usually about people in the news at the time or about the place the pantomime is being performed in. It also gets the audience involved, usually shouting 'He's behind you' or 'Oh yes you did' to a character involved in the action.

In this section you are going to think about how a piece of written script can become a real, knockabout pantomime on the stage. The following extract is taken from a version of one of the most famous pantomimes, *Dick Whittington*.

Dick is on board ship, bound for the mythical land of Montonia along with Alice, her father (Fitzwarren), Idle Jack, Captain Cockle and Mr Mussel the Mate. The ship is sunk by the 'baddy' of the pantomime, King Rat, and Dick thinks that all his friends have been drowned. He and his cat are brought in front of the Sultan, who is desperately trying to rid Montonia of a plague of rats.

Assignment 1

As a group, decide what each character is like. Remember that characters in pantomimes are always very exaggerated and larger than life.

Decide who is going to play each character.

Assignment 2

Decide what clothes each character will wear during this scene. Describe in detail for each what you would like the wardrobe department to provide. Remember that pantomimes are very colourful and think about the visual impact you would like each to make on stage. Also think about the period of the clothes you want. Pantomimes are set in mythical places at no real time in history, which gives you a lot of freedom in deciding what characters can wear.

Assignment 3

Decide how you would perform this extract.

To start with just sit down and practise reading your lines together from the script, concentrating on getting the timing right and plenty of exaggerated expression in your voice. Make sure the corny jokes come over!

If you have time, learn your lines and your cues. Cues are the lines that come before yours. You need to know these as well so that, when you haven't got the script in front of you, you know when to speak your lines.

When you are all confident about your characters and lines, start working out how to move around the stage. The stage directions in brackets in the script will help you here.

WERAFEZ *(announcing)* His Imperial Magnificence, the Sultan of Montonia!
EL MACHO And Tuffazell, the Keeper of the Slaves!

Fanfare, all fall to the floor, including the Guards, and prostrate themselves

ALL *(on the floor)* Salaam! Salaam!

Tuffazell, the Keeper of the Slaves, enters backwards, salaaming her arms up and down, and the Sultan follows

SULTAN You have my gracious permission to rise.

All get up

TUFFAZELL Loyal greetings, Your Significance!
SULTAN Never mind the greetings, what about the squeakings?
TUFFAZELL The squeakings, Your Exorbitance?
SULTAN Those terrible rats – what news of them?
TUFFAZELL How should I know, Your Effervescence?
SULTAN Because you're the Wazir – and you was here!

All laugh. Tuffazell makes a chopping gesture with her hands and shouts out a command

TUFFAZELL *(a female sergeant-major)* Silence you slobbering insignificant slaves! To the kitchens – to the horrible rats! Imshi! Imshi!

All bow and exit fast, leaving the Sultan and Tuffazell

SULTAN *(desperate)* Oh these rats! You must issue a royal proclamation – tell the whole living world – and *(some ridiculous sounding local place)* – that I will give half my gold and jewels to anyone that can rid my kingdom of the rats!

TUFFAZELL Your command shall be obeyed, Your Protuberance.
SULTAN Don't be cheeky – you are insultin' the Sultan.
TUFFAZELL Apologies, Your Imperial Leather.

The two Guards enter

SULTAN Ah, Werafez!

Werafez bows

And you, El Macho!

The second Guard bows

What news?
WERAFEZ Sayida afeed fahradan danoon!
SULTAN *(interested)* Are you serious?
EL MACHO *(nodding his head)* Nooshivah achmandan!
SULTAN Then show him in at once!

The Guards bow and exit

TUFFAZELL But is this wise? He is someone from England, Your Circumference! A barbarian!
SULTAN From *England*? Then you may have to prepare the boiling oil for a lingering death. Are you strong enough to manage that?
TUFFAZELL *(offended)* Strong enough? It was I that tore in half the Montonian Telephone Directory!
SULTAN True. True. Ah!

Werafez ushers in Dick and exits, while Dick strides forward cheerfully

DICK Your Superbness! *(A cheeky salute)* Hi!
TUFFAZELL *(outraged)* Bow to His Majesty, you English infidel!
DICK *(as he bows)* Apologies to you both. May I introduce you to my friend, Tommy?
TUFFAZELL *(laughing in a superior way)* 'Tommy'? These ugly English words! Ha ha ha – *(She sees Tommy entering and stops laughing, as she becomes petrified)* Waaaah!

Tommy enters. Both the Sultan and Tuffazell register total terror – Tuffazell jumps up and down and stamps her feet in fright

SULTAN	What terrible beast is this?
DICK	*(laughing)* Your Majesty, I'm Dick Whittington, and this is my cat!
SULTAN	*(staring at Tommy)* Mycat! I've never heard of a mycat.

Tommy creeps across watched by the nervous Sultan and Tuffazell

DICK	He's harmless, your Majesty! He won't hurt you – will you Tommy?

Tommy shakes his head

> Your Majesty, may I present my cat Tommy – Tommy, this is the Great Ruler, the Imperial Majesty, the Mighty Sultan of Montonia!

Tommy salutes cheerfully

TOMMY	Meeeow!
SULTAN	*(stepping back a pace)* G-g-good-afternoon.
DICK	Honestly sir, he's not a bit dangerous! Tommy, shake hands with the Sultan.

Tommy holds out his paw. The Sultan is nervous, so is Tuffazell

> Go on sir – it's all right! Shake paws!

They shake hands

SULTAN *(to Tommy)* So you're a mycat. Welcome to Montonia.

Tommy bows

DICK	Welcome indeed Your Majesty – because cats are the one thing that rats are scared of!
SULTAN	*(delighted)* They are? Splendid! *(To Tommy)* So you're going to help me get rid of the rats?

Tommy nods and does some 'shadow boxing'. The Sultan and Tuffazell laugh, relieved Werafez the Guard enters

WERAFEZ	Your Majesty, some miserable prisoners!

Jack, the Captain, the Mate, Alice and Fitzwarren enter much frightened, wailing loudly as they kneel in a line facing the Sultan and Tuffazell

ALL	*(raising their arms in the air)* Woe! Woe! Oh woe!
TUFFAZELL	Be quiet!
CAPTAIN	*(urgently to his Mate)* Stay on your knees and plead.
MATE	What?
CAPTAIN	*Plead.* You should be pleading.
MATE	But I haven't cut myself!

Tuffazell	Silence! You are spies, and in Montonia, spies have their heads cut off.
Jack	Oh don't cut my head off! I'll have nowhere to put my hat!
Sultan	*(to Fitzwarren)* How would *you* like to die?
Fitzwarren	Of old age! But I wouldn't mind a suspended sentence.
Sultan	A splendid idea – I'll hang you.
Tuffazell	*(her odd deep contralto laugh)* Har har har har har! *(She shakes with laughter)*
Fitzwarren	Couldn't you just shoot me at dawn?
Sultan	Impossible. I don't get up till eight.
Mate	*(defiantly)* If you shoot *me*, I'll never speak to you again.
Tuffazell	Silence, you English idiot!
Mate	How dare you call me English!
Sultan	*(evilly)* Before you are exterminated, have you any last requests?
Jack	*(cheerfully)* Yes, this one is for Uncle Harry, Auntie Freda, Gran and Grandad at number eight Greenfield Avenue and I'd like to hear Boy George singing – *(aghast)* – what am I saying?
Sultan	You are saying things that I do not like to hear. *(Threatening them all)* You have been brought here to die.
Captain	No – it was yesterdie. *(Explaining)* That's when we got here – I was washed up.
Sultan	And by the look of things you're *still* washed up. *(Loudly)* You are all going to die!
Dick	Your Majesty, you must spare them! They're my friends! I thought you were *pleased* about me and my cat?
Tommy	*(paws held together in prayer, and kneeling upright)* Meeeow!
Sultan	*(to Tommy)* All right. The mycat may save my kingdom from the rats. *(Grandly)* Because of the mycat, you shall be free!

Great relief and the prisoners stand up

Alice	*(relieved, running across to Dick)* Dick – you and Tommy have saved us!
Sultan	*(expansively)* Come! You shall be shown round my palace by the Keeper of my Slaves. *(He points to her)* She is Tuffazell.
Jack	You're telling me!
Tuffazell	Silence - or I shall cut off your legs and call you shorty.
Jack	Oooooh!
Tuffazell	*(to all)* Come this way – to the Courtyard of the Fifteen Fountains!

She ushers them out and all exit chattering. Last to go are Jack and Tuffazell

Tuffazell	*(to Jack, flirtatiously)* You mustn't worry. When I shout at you it means I *like* you.
Jack	*(in horror)* AAAAAGH!

FOCUS ON
Poetry

A poet's view

Poet Gillian Clark tells us what she feels poetry is all about:

Most people enjoy words, and poetry of one sort or another: nursery rhymes, playground games, dipping and skipping rhymes, ring-games, rock lyrics, nonsense verse, television jingles, limericks, or what poets like Ted Hughes or Shakespeare write. Take your pick. Poetry is natural, and when you were babies you all loved it.

A poem should give you pleasure, a little shiver of recognition, as if you and the poem have met before. It should excite or scare you a little, set you thinking or help you understand something you didn't understand before. When you've read it, or heard it, you should remember parts of it, a line, a phrase, or an image.

If none of this happens something is wrong. It may be the wrong poem for you, you are in the wrong mood, or you are shutting it out, perhaps because you think it is difficult and that you are going to have to work at it and answer questions about it. When I write a poem I might want to make you work a little, but most of all I want a reader to say, 'Yes! I've felt like that.'

There's a very old woman from my village whose grandfather was killed by a highwayman. It is a sad and wicked story, but it gives me a shiver of excitement, and I'm sure that's due to 'The Highwayman' by Alfred Noyes, my favourite poem when I was a child. It begins,

> **'The wind was a torrent of darkness among the gusty trees.
> The moon was a ghostly galleon tossed upon cloudy seas.'**

To this day I see the moon in fast-moving cloud as a ghostly galleon, and as I lie listening to the wind the whole poem comes back to me. I also enjoyed the solemn rhythm of 'The Burial of Sir John Moore at Corunna', by Charles Wolfe.

> **'Not a drum was heard, not a funeral note,
> As his corse to the rampart we hurried'.**

Poems have tunes, and they have mysteries. The mystery word here is 'corse', an old word for 'corpse'. The poet writes that, when they had buried the body, they 'smoothed down his lonely pillow'. That's a metaphor, two things put together in a surprising way to produce a sudden and unexpected picture in the mind. The 'lonely pillow' is really the grave. Poets have called the shoe of a great carthorse a 'bright and battering sandal', grasshoppers 'the guns of August', a new lamb's coat a 'cardigan'.

Such images make the world new, and, like the tunes and mysteries of poetry, never leave your mind.

8: Poetry and Posters

Useful Person

We'd missed the train. Two hours to wait
On Lime Street Station, Liverpool,
With *not a single thing to do*.
The bar was shut and Dad was blue
And Mum was getting in a state
And everybody felt a fool.

Yes, we were very glum indeed.
Myself, I'd nothing new to read,
No sweets to eat, no game to play.
'I'm bored,' I said, and straight away,
Mum said what I knew she'd say:
'Go on, then, read a book, OK?'
'I've *read* them *both!*' 'That's no excuse.'

Dad sat sighing, '*What* a day ...
This is precious little use.
I wish they'd open up that bar.'
They didn't, though. No way.

And everybody else was sitting
In the waiting-room and knitting,
Staring, scratching, yawning, smoking.
'All right, Dad?' 'You must be joking!
This is precious little use.
It's like a prison. Turn me loose!'

('Big fool, act your age!' Mum hisses.
'Sorry, missus.'
'Worse than him, you are,' said Mum.)

It was grim. It was glum.

And then the Mongol child came up,
Funny-faced:
Something in her body wrong,
Something in her mind
Misplaced:

Something in her eyes was strange:
What, or why, I couldn't tell:
But somehow she was beautiful
As well.

Anyway, she took us over!
'Hello, love,' said Dad. She said,
'There, sit *there!'* and punched a spot
On the seat. The spot was what,
Almost, Mum was sitting on,
So Dad squeezed up, and head-to-head,
And crushed-up, hip-to-hip, they sat.
'What next, then?' *'Kiss!'* 'Oh no, not that!'
Dad said, chuckling. *'Kiss!'*
                            They did!
I thought my Mum would flip her lid
With laughing. Then the Mongol child
Was filled with pleasure – she went wild,
Running round the tables, telling
Everyone to *kiss* and yelling
Out to everyone to sit
Where she said. They did, too. It
Was sudden happiness because
The Mongol child
Was what she was:
Bossy, happy, full of fun,
And just *determined* everyone
Should have a good time too! We knew
That's what we'd got to do.

Goodness me, she took us over!
All the passengers for Dover,
Wolverhampton, London, Crewe –
Everyone from everywhere
Began to share
Her point of view! The more they
   squeezed,
And laughed, and fooled about, the
   more

The Mongol child
Was pleased!

Dad had to kiss another Dad
('Watch it, lad!' 'You watch it, lad!'
'Stop: you're not my kind of bloke!')
Laugh? I thought my Mum would
   choke!

And so the time whirled by. The train
Whizzed us home again
And on the way I thought of her:
Precious little use is what
Things had been. Then she came
And things were not
The same!

She was precious, she was little,
She was useful too:
Made us speak when we were dumb,
Made us smile when we were blue,
Cheered us up when we were glum,
Lifted us when we were flat:
Who could be
More use than that?

Mongol child,
Funny-faced,
Something in your body wrong,
Something in your mind
Misplaced,
Something in your eyes, strange:
What, or why, I cannot tell:
I thought you were beautiful:

Useful, as well.

▼ Assignment 1

Please note that Down's Syndrome is the accepted term to describe these children, not Mongol, which is not used nowadays.

1 What was the poet's first reaction to the girl with Down's Syndrome?
2 Why did she manage to make everyone do what she wanted?
3 The phrase 'precious little use' occurs at both the beginning and the end of the poem. How is its meaning different in each place?
4 What message do you think the poet is trying to get across about the child?

▼ Assignment 2

The two posters that follow have been produced by the Down's Syndrome Association and the Down's Children's Association. Think about the reasons for such posters. Why does a group like this need to advertise?
Then look carefully at the poster of Sarah and answer the following questions:

1 Does it attract your attention? How does it try to do this?
2 What do you think the caption is trying to tell you?
3 Does it make you stop and think? About what?
4 What do the poster and the poem have in common?

Study the other poster, and answer the following:

1 How does this poster try to capture your interest?
2 What do you think of the caption? Is it more important than the picture?
3 Which poster do you prefer? Is one more powerful than the other? Why, or why not?
4 Have the posters and poem changed the way you think about these children in any way? If they have, explain how they have done this.
5 Do the posters say anything that the poem doesn't, or vice versa?

8:2 Uncle Edward

Uncle Edward's Affliction

Uncle Edward was colour-blind;
We grew accustomed to the fact.
When he asked someone to hand him
The green book from the window-seat
And we observed its bright red cover
Either apathy or tact
Stifled comment. We passed it over.
Much later, I began to wonder
What curious world he wandered in,
Down streets where pea-green pillar boxes
Grinned at a fire engine as green;
How Uncle Edward's sky at dawn
And sunset flooded marshy green.
Did he ken John Peel with his coat so green
And Robin Hood in Lincoln red?
On country walks avoid being stung
By nettles hot as a witch's tongue?
What meals he savoured with his eyes:
Green strawberries and fresh red peas,
Green beef and greener burgundy.
All unscientific, so it seems:
His world was not at all like that,
So those who claim to know have said.
Yet, I believe, in war-smashed France
He must have crawled from neutral mud
To lie in pastures dark and red
And seen, appalled, on every blade
The rain of innocent green blood.

VERNON SCANNELL

Vernon Scannell wrote this about this poem:

'Uncle Edward's Affliction' is intended to express something of my admiration for the generation which fought in the filth and carnage of the trenches of the 1914 – 1918 war. It is not factual in that I do not possess an Uncle Edward who is colour-blind. But I once met a young husband and wife who did have an uncle – I don't know his name – and he was, they told me, 'an irritating old bore'. When I asked why he was so boring and irritating they said, 'He's colour-blind and he will go on about the First World War. He's obsessed by it. Always talking about being wounded on the Somme.' Well, as you will see by the poem, my sympathy was entirely with the old man.

▼ Assignment 1

Read the poem to yourself once or twice, and then answer the questions that follow. They will help you to understand the poem, which you will need to do before going on to assignment 2.

1. What was Uncle Edward's affliction?
2. What was the poet's attitude towards it when he was young?
3. How did this change as he grew older?
4. Why does the poet mention John Peel and Robin Hood?
5. What are the last five lines of the poem about?
6. Why do you think the poet uses the phrase 'innocent green blood'? What meaning, other than the colour, do we give to the word green? If we say someone is green, what do we mean?
7. How does the mood of the poem change at the end? The word mood is used to explain how the poem is supposed to make you feel when you are reading it. A person can be in a good mood or bad, angry or sad, and a poem can reflect these emotions in its mood.
8. Judging from the poem, what did the poet think of Uncle Edward? How do you know?

▼ Assignment 2

As a group, prepare a reading of this poem for a radio programme. Decide how many readers you require, and then work on the way this poem should be read aloud. Think carefully about the expression that is required for each line, and, if you have more than one reader, who will read which lines.

Pictures in Words

Baking Day

Thursday was baking day in our house.
The spicy smell of new baked bread would meet
My nostrils when I came home from school and there would be
Fresh buns for tea, but better still were the holidays.

Then I could stay and watch the baking of the bread.
My mother would build up the fire and pull out the damper
Until the flames were flaring under the oven; while it was heating
She would get out her earthenware bowl and baking board.

Into the crater of flour in the bowl she would pour sugar
And yeast in hot water; to make sure the yeast was fresh
I had often been sent to fetch it from the grocer that morning,
And it smelt of the earth after rain as it dissolved in the sweet water.

Then her small stubby hands would knead and pummel
The dough until they became two clowns in baggy pantaloons,
And the right one, whose three fingers and blue stump
Told of the accident which followed my birth, became whole.

As the hands worked a creamy elastic ball
Took shape and covered by a white cloth was set
On a wooden chair by the fire slowly to rise:
To me the most mysterious rite of all.

From time to time I would peep at the living dough
To make sure it was not creeping out of the bowl.
Sometimes I imagined it possessed, filling the whole room,
And we helpless, unable to control its power to grow.

But as it heaved above the rim of the bowl mother
Was there taking it and moulding it into plaited loaves
And buns and giving me a bit to make into a bread man,
With currant eyes, and I, too, was a baker.

My man was baked with the loaves and I would eat him for tea.
On Friday night, when the plaited loaves were placed
Under a white napkin on the dining table,
Beside two lighted candles, they became holy.

No bread will ever be so full of the sun as the pieces
We were given to eat after prayers and the cutting of the bread.
My mother, who thought her life had been narrow, did not want
Her daughters to be bakers of bread. I think she was wise.

Yet sometimes, when my cultivated brain chafes at kitchen
Tasks, I remember her, patiently kneading dough
And rolling pastry, her untutored intelligence
All bent towards nourishing her children.

ROSEMARY JOSEPH

▼ Assignment 1

Many poems rely for their effect on the way they use a few words to create a striking picture in the reader's mind. Read this poem carefully and try to match the pictures below to the relevant verse. The pictures are an artist's impression of the images that the poet has drawn with words.

An image is a picture or impression or feeling, created by an author, poet, musician or artist in a work of art. (The word image is derived from the Latin word *imago*, meaning a copy or representation.) In this case the picture is painted with words.

▼ Assignment 2

Now look at the following phrases, which create images in a reader's mind. What do you see when you read them?

new baked bread, smelt of the earth living dough, plaited loaves, full of the sun, patiently kneading dough

Look carefully at the last six images – are they all supposed to be visual, or are any of them different?

▼ Assignment 3

Look carefully at the last two verses of the poem. As a group, try to decide what they mean. Is this poem just about a child watching her mother bake bread? What else do you think it could be about?

▼ Assignment 4

Choose three parts of the poem that you enjoyed, and explain why. If you did not like the poem, explain as fully as possible why not.

8.4 Haiku

A haiku is a special type of poem. It has a set pattern to it and is only three lines long. In the poem on the pages before this the poet has tried to paint a word-picture, and that is exactly what a haiku does, but in a different way.

A haiku is made up of three lines, the first with five syllables in, the second with seven and the third with five syllables again. A syllable is the name given to a part of a word that contains a single vowel sound. 'Sun' is one syllable and 'shine' is another, so that 'sunshine' is a two-syllable word. The word 'haiku' is made up of two syllables. Read the word aloud *(high-koo)*. Can you hear the two syllables?

▼ **Assignment 1**

Look at the two haiku following, and count the syllables in each line.

Child

Sunshine is your smile,
Lighting up my life with love
More and more each day.

Saturdays

Like given sweet coins
The first summer-sea paddle
Or the first real kiss.

The first haiku has a metaphor in it –
that is, something is said to be
something else. Can you find it?

The second haiku has a simile in it –
that is, something is said to be as or like
something else.

Now write some haiku about things
that you like or about one or two of the
following pictures.

8:5 Inventing words

Jabberwocky

'Twas brillig, and the slithy toves
Did gyre and gimble in the wabe ;
All mimsy were the borogoves ,
And the mome raths outgrabe.

'Beware the Jabberwock, my son!
The jaws that bite, the claws that catch!
Beware the Jubjub bird, and shun
The frumious Bandersnatch!'

He took his vorpal sword in hand:
Long time the manxome foe he sought
So rested he by the Tumtum tree,
And stood awhile in thought.

And as in uffish thought he stood,
The Jabberwock, with eyes of flame,
Came whiffling through the tulgey wood,
And burbled as it came!

One, two! One, two! And through and through
The vorpal blade went snicker-snack!
He left it dead, and with its head
He went galumphing back.

'And hast thou slain the Jabberwock?
Come to my arms, my beamish boy!
O frabjous day! Callooh! Callay!'
He chortled in his joy.

'Twas brillig, and the slithy toves
Did gyre and gimble in the wabe;
All mimsy were the borogoves,
And the mome raths outgrabe.

LEWIS CARROLL

The poem 'Jabberwocky' first appeared in *Alice through the Looking Glass*, a story by Lewis Carroll. Many of the words in the poem were made up by Lewis Carroll.

Read the poem, possibly aloud around your group, to get a feel for it.

'Jabberwocky' works because Lewis Carroll left in many words which we can understand, and the made-up words still fit into their right place in the structure of the sentence. We understand, often without realising it, the structure of our language.

For instance, let's take the first line of the poem:

'Twas brillig, and the slithy toves

"'Twas' is an old-fashioned (archaic) way of saying 'it was'. The word following it does not have an 'a' or 'the' before it, so it can only be a time ('It was four o'clock') or a word telling us what type of day it was ('It was fine').

'Slithy' is used like an adjective to describe 'toves', and toves are obviously things that can 'gyre and gimble' in the wabe. So 'toves' are nouns and 'gyre and gimble' are verbs.

▼ Assignment 1

Look at the words in boxes. What do you think they mean? Try to think of some actual words that could replace them.

▼ Assignment 2

Now look at the other nonsense words and at the replacement words you've thought of. Can you say whether the nonsense words are nouns, verbs or adjectives?

▼ Assignment 3

1 Write a poem of your own. You could copy the format of 'Jabberwocky' by having verses of four lines each. Try to make up some unusual words as Lewis Carroll did, but don't get carried away or people won't be able to understand it.

2 Make a secret list of the meanings and then ask your friends to write down what they think the real meanings of your words are. Make sure you give your words the correct form and ending depending on whether they are nouns, verbs or adjectives.

▼ Assignment 4

'Jabberwocky' is an interesting example of how new words can come into the language. If enough people start using them, made-up words can become 'real' ones. This happened to one word in the poem – 'galumphing'. Look it up in your dictionary to see how it's defined now.

9 ▶ FOCUS ON Fiction

What attracts you to a book? Is it: the attractive cover? the title of the book? the name of the author? the type of story it is?

What advice would you give to someone who finds it hard to choose a book?

Thomas:
Read a bit of the book before you decide to borrow it.

Clare:
Read the paragraph on the back of the book as this gives you a good idea of what it is about.

Ian:
Find an author that you like and read all his or her books.

Jessica:
Choose a short book with a good storyline.

Joanne:
Choose a book about a subject you like and read that.

Matthew:
Borrow a friend's favourite book.

Claire:
Look at the title of the book and see if it sounds promising.

David:
Look for an exciting and adventurous book with maybe a good author.

Why do you like reading?

Heidi:
The thing I like about reading is that it makes me feel as if I'm part of the book and it's all happening to me.

Danielle:
There is nothing else to do. I'm a bookworm.

Mark:
I find it interesting and it triggers my imagination.

Matthew:
The entertainment.

Elaine:
The thing I like is how some of the authors write their books and some of the books are really exciting.

Diane:
That when I'm reading a book I really get stuck in and imagine that *I'm* there.

Annamarie:
I like the quietness and it's good to be on your own sometimes.

Fiction

James:
You can imagine how you want the character to be.

Jessica:
You can read any time of the day.

Yacub:
It gives you time to yourself.

Paul:
It is nice to read in bed.

Deesha:
It takes you on an adventure.

Laura:
Some books mix fiction with nonfiction. Cynthia Harnett is good at that and I enjoy those.

Becky:
Books let me escape into the characters' lives.

Luke:
I like finding out new things.

Joanne:
I like reading before I turn the light out – it gives me something to think about.

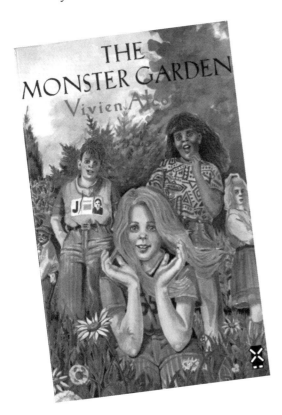

▼ **Over to you**

What do you look for in a book?

Do you enjoy reading? If so, why? If not, why not?

9 Conrad the Factory Made Boy

Read the passage that follows carefully and then answer the questions.

Mrs Bartolotti, the woman you will read about in the passage, has a habit of ordering things from catalogues and papers. She orders so many things this way that often she can't remember what she has ordered, and sometimes when it arrives she has a big shock.

THESE GOODS HAVE BEEN EXAMINED SEVERAL TIMES AND LEFT OUR WAREHOUSE IN PERFECT CONDITION.

Mrs Bartolotti put the letter and the envelope down on the kitchen table, bent over the carton and began rummaging around among the sky-blue shavings. She could feel something smooth, hard and cold under them. She flung them out of the carton and then she saw a huge, gleaming, silvery tin can. It was about the height of a gentleman's umbrella, and was as thick as the trunk of a thirty-year-old tree. There was no label on the tin can, only a sky-blue dot about the size of a five pence piece. One end of the can had TOP on it and the other end had BOTTOM, and there were letters round the middle of the can saying: *All documents will be found inside.*

Mrs Bartolotti rolled the tin can out of its carton and stood it upright, so that the end saying TOP was on top and the end saying BOTTOM was on the bottom. She rapped the side of the tin can; it sounded hollow. 'Can't be fruit cocktail, then', she muttered.

'Could be popcorn', she added.

Mrs Bartolotti was very fond of popcorn. But when she took a closer look at the can she realised it couldn't be popcorn either. Indeed, it could not contain anything that was runny or crumbly, because it was the kind of can which has a strip of metal all round the middle and a ring-pull to open it. If you pull the ring you can rip off the strip of metal all the way round and the two halves of the can come apart. So obviously there was something solid inside this tin can!

'Corned beef!' said Mrs Bartolotti to herself, taking hold of the ring-pull. Mrs Bartolotti liked corned beef even better than popcorn. Twenty kilos of corned beef are rather a lot, and Mrs Bartolotti knew she could never get all that into her refrigerator, but she thought: Never mind, I'll give a kilo to Thomas, and I'll give old Mrs Miller another kilo, and I'll give little Micky two, and I shall send three kilos to dear old Uncle Albert express delivery! At least that will show him I'm thinking of him more than he's thinking of me. What's more, I shan't have to go shopping for a whole week, thought Mrs Barolotti. I'll have corned beef for breakfast and lunch and tea and supper... And she pulled the ring.

'You leave that alone, my dear... something might go wrong', a voice whispered in her left ear.

Fiction

'Oh do hurry up and get this funny can open, my dear!' a voice whispered in her right ear. But since both voices were her own, Mrs Bartolotti did not take them seriously. In any case, it was too late by now; at least five centimetres of metal strip had come away already. Mrs Bartolotti went on pulling. There was a funny hissing sound. When Mrs Barolotti had quite finished pulling off the metal strip the top half of the can was hanging askew over the bottom half, and the hissing stopped. There was a smell of carbolic and hospitals and fresh, ozone-laden air.

'That's no way for corned beef to smell. Unless it's very poor quality corned beef', muttered Mrs Bartolotti, lifting the top half of the tin can.

It was a very good thing the kitchen stool was right behind Mrs Bartolotti, because she got a considerable shock. She started trembling from the bleached ends of her hair down to her toenails, which were varnished bright green. She felt rather dizzy. She swayed, and collapsed on to the kitchen stool.

The creature who was crouching inside the tin can said, 'Hullo, Mummy', and gave her a friendly nod.

This is taken from *Conrad the Factory Made Boy* by Christine Nostlinger, published by Heinemann Educational, if you would like to read it in full.

9:1

▼ **Assignment 1**

1. What did Mrs Bartolotti think might be inside the tin can, and why? Do her ideas about the contents of the tin tell you anything about her?
2. What did Mrs Bartolotti plan to do with all the corned beef that she thought was in the tin?
3. What do you think of the way she reacted to the possibility that she might have 20 kilos of corned beef to get rid of? What does this tell you about her?
4. What does the writer mean by the line 'But since both voices were her own, Mrs Bartolotti did not take them seriously'?
5. Mrs Bartolotti was not sure whether to open the can or not. Explain how you would have felt if you had been there, and why. Why would you have opened it or not opened it?

▼ **Assignment 2**

Imagine that you lived next door to Mrs Bartolotti and that you were trying to explain what she was like to another friend. Use information from the passage and some of your previous answers to help you write as much as you can about her personality and appearance.

▼ **Assignment 3**

Look at the verbs and adjectives that the author of this extract has used. If you look just at the last paragraph you will find verbs like 'trembling', 'varnished', 'swayed' and 'collapsed', and adjectives like 'considerable'. Why do these words make the writing more interesting?

Look at the following version of the first paragraph without adjectives or interesting verbs. Which version would you prefer to have written?

Mrs Bartolotti put the letter and the envelope down on the table, bent over the carton and looked around among the shavings. She could feel something under them. She took them out of the carton and she saw a tin can. It was about 1 metre high and 35 cm across. There was no label on the can, only a dot. One end of the can had TOP on it, and the other end had BOTTOM, and there were letters around the middle of the can saying: *All documents will be found inside.*

▼ Assignment 4

1 Look at the list of adjectives that follow. They are all words that you can use to describe people's appearance.

Put them into categories. Start with words you could use to describe someone's hair and work downwards. Some words describe a person's character and some describe the whole person's physical appearance.

2 As a class, make a list of verbs you could use to describe how someone talks and walks.

3 Now with your partner look at the description you wrote of Mrs Bartolotti. Try to see how together you could improve your assignments by rewriting them and using some more interesting verbs and adjectives than you have done.

long, ruby-red, domed, small, big, pointy, round, elf-like, slender, short, fat, podgy, broad, muscular, wavy, thick, lustrous, shiny, golden, raven, short, tousled, wide, curvy, heavy, slender, knobbly, hairy, bulbous, hooked, Roman, happy, grinning, sad, ugly, depressed, pretty, haggard, flabby, wrinkled, grotesque, slim, agile, lithe, gaunt, angular, delicate, strong, frail, statuesque, tall, gangly, elegant, clumsy, rosy, turned-up, moody, angry, suspicious, confident, short-tempered, crazy, shady, cautious, confiding, childish, kind, generous, sympathetic, threatening, thoughtful, friendly, hostile, solitary, curious, gregarious, bright, miserable, cheerful, likeable, popular, wet, tough, brutal, enthusiastic, excitable, imaginative, pleasant, naughty, irritable, stupid, clever, macho

9:2 Summer's End

I could hear the milk-cart in the street. The horse, Bugger, stamped his feet irritably every time it had to stop. I knew the horse was called Bugger because that's what the milkman called him.

'Hey, you Bugger. Give over... Hold on a bit, Bugger... Whoa, you Bugger.'

I lay in bed and could hear Bugger's iron-clad feet clipping the tarmac like four giant ice-skates. Sometimes he snorted and the sound came to me like wind blowing in a chimney. The sounds of the milk-urns were thin as tinsel for the empty ones and solid-thick for the full ones. I lay abed, sharing with two brothers, and wouldn't open my eyes. I tried to make my ears tell me things. I made them pierce the bedroom walls and stand in the street to let me know if it was raining outside. They couldn't hear any sounds of rain but I mistrusted them. It *had* to rain today because I didn't want it to. I tried to make my ears read the sky for sounds of clouds, rain-clouds, bumping into each other like bullies in a playground. I tried to make my ears listen for the sizzling sound of sunlight, like bacon frizzling in a pan. My ears were liars because they told me nothing, and that's the biggest lie anybody or anything can tell. The lie of silence; which doesn't exist.

I didn't open my eyes. I stretched them. Stretched my eyelids. The dark purple of tight-shut eyes gave way to warmer red. I held that colour and tried to examine it. Streaks of lighter colours painted across my lids, flower-colours. I stretched them a bit more and there was golden yellow, the colour of pollen sticking to a bumble-bee's belly. I took a deep breath and opened my eyes. Sunlight snatched them towards the bedroom window, and the dazzle of the blue sky brought me fully awake. I climbed out of bed and went to the window and it was a fête-day of summer warmth and sunlight. It pleased me the same as pop does when it tingles bubbles at the back of your nose. It was a glorious day and not a threat of wet-clouds anywhere. The narrow street was dusty with sunlight, so rich that even the dark shadows it couldn't reach took some heed of the sun-glow and mellowed into warm mahogany.

Bugger, the milk-horse, was letting the shafts of the cart hold him up while he swished flies away from his back-end with sweeps of his tail. He looked bored to death. He wouldn't be happy until the round was done and the leathers and chains taken from him, the huge collar hung on its peg in the stable, and he himself turned into the fenced freedom of his paddock. Two or three of our women were clustered round the cart with their platter jugs. The milkman was standing in the cart, plunging his long dipper into one of the tall urns and then pouring the snow-whiteness into the jugs. As they went away up their entries to their back-kitchens the milkman took a stub of pencil from behind his ear, wetted it with the tip of his tongue, and wrote their owings into his tally-book. The women would settle with him come Saturday dinner-time, when their men got paid. The window sashes creaked and complained bitterly as I pushed the bottom window up and stuck my head out.

'Good morning, Bugger', I shouted down. The milkman looked up at me.

'I'll bugger you, if I get my hands on you', he said, 'you cheeky young sod.'

This is taken from *Summer's End* by Archie Hill.

Read the story and enjoy it.

▼ Assignment 1

1 Pick out all the descriptions that have 'as' or 'like' in them; for example, 'iron-clad feet clipping the tarmac like four giant ice-skates'. Why is this a good way of writing descriptions?

Look at the way these sentences are written. They are called similes. Look back to page 85 for a definition of a simile.

2 Pick out all the interesting verbs and adjectives the writer has used to describe the day, and discuss them in your group. Explain what they tell you about the day and how the boy felt. Use a dictionary to look up any words you don't understand.

When you write a story it is important to use language that makes it interesting, especially when you are describing settings and characters. The better the picture you paint with words, the easier it is for the reader to imagine it.

▼ Assignment 2

Write your own story, based on an incident that you can remember from your childhood. Remember that your first piece of writing can be improved, and be prepared to produce two or three drafts until you are happy with it.

9:3 The Sheep-Pig

This passage is taken from a book called *The Sheep-Pig*, which is about a very unusual animal.

In the following assignments you will be working out what's happening in the passage and looking at some of the ways it uses language.

First of all, read the passage.

What happened next, later that morning in fact, was that Babe met his first sheep.

Farmer Hogget and Fly had been out round the flock, and when they returned Fly was driving before her an old lame ewe, which they penned in the loose-box where the piglet had originally been shut. Then they went away up the hill again.

Babe made his way into the stables, curious to meet this, the first of the animals that he planned one day to work with, but he could not see into the box. He snuffled under the bottom of the door, and from inside there came a cough and the sharp stamp of a foot, and then the sound of a hoarse complaining voice. 'Wolves! Wolves!' it said. 'They do never leave a body alone. Nag, nag, nag all day long, go here, go there, do this, do that. What d'you want now? Can't you give us a bit of peace, wolf?'

'I'm not a wolf', said Babe under the door.

'Oh, I knows all that', said the sheep sourly. 'Calls yourself a sheep-dog, I knows that, but you don't fool none of us. You're a wolf like the rest of 'em, given half a chance. You looks at us, and you sees lamb-chops. Go away, wolf.'

'But I'm not a sheep-dog either', said Babe, and he scrambled up the stack of straw bales and looked over the bars.

'You see?' he said.

'Well I'll be dipped', said the old sheep, peering at him, 'no more you ain't. What are you?'

'Pig', said Babe. 'Large White. What are you?'

'Ewe', said the sheep.

'No, not me, you – what are you?'

'I'm a ewe.'

Mum was right, thought Babe, they certainly are stupid. But if I'm going to learn how to be a sheep-pig I must try to understand them, and this might be a good chance. Perhaps I could make a friend of this one.

'My name's Babe', he said in a jolly voice. 'What's yours?'

'Maaaaa', said the sheep.

'That's a nice name,' said Babe. 'What's the matter with you, Ma?'

'Foot-rot', said the sheep, holding up a foreleg. 'And I've got a nasty cough.' She coughed. 'And I'm not as young as I was.'

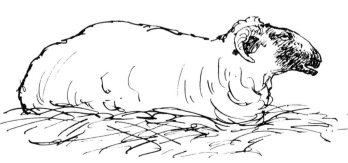

'You don't look very old to me,' said Babe politely.

A look of pleasure came over the sheep's mournful face, and she lay down in the straw.

'Very civil of you to say so', she said. 'First kind word I've had since I were a little lamb', and she belched loudly and began to chew a mouthful of cud.

Though he did not quite know why, Babe said nothing to Fly of his conversation with Ma. Farmer Hogget had treated the sheep's foot and tipped a drench down its protesting throat, and now, as darkness fell, dog and pig lay side by side, their rest only occasionally disturbed by a rustling from the next-door box. Having at last set eyes on a sheep, Babe's dreams were immediately filled with the creatures, all lame, all coughing, all, like the ducks, scattering wildly before his attempts to round them up.

'Go here, go there, do this, do that!' he squeaked furiously at them, but they took not a bit of notice, until at last the dream turned to nightmare, and they all came hopping and hacking and maa-ing after him with hatred gleaming in their mad yellow eyes.

'Mum! Mum!' shouted Babe in terror.

'Maaaaa!' said a voice next door.

'It's all right, dear', said Fly, 'it's all right. Was it a nasty dream?'

'Yes, yes.'

'What were you dreaming about?'

'Sheep, Mum.'

'I expect it was because of that stupid old thing in there', said Fly. 'Shut up!' she barked. 'Noisy old fool!' And to Babe she said, 'Now cuddle up, dear, and go to sleep. There's nothing to be frightened of.'

This is taken from *The Sheep-Pig* by Dick King-Smith.

9:3

▼ Assignment 1

1. What sorts of animal are Fly and Babe?
2. Why do you think Babe calls her Mum?
3. Why does Babe want to meet a sheep?
4. Why had the old sheep been penned up in the loose-box?
5. Why did Babe think that the sheep was stupid?
6. What is the sheep's view of Babe and why does it change?
7. What differences are there in the way Fly treats Babe and the way she treats the sheep?

▼ Assignment 2

The sheep talks in a form of sheep dialect. A dialect is a form of English with words and word structure which are peculiar to itself. For example, the sheep calls sheep-dogs 'wolves'. It also has its own form of verb structures; for example: 'They do never leave...' and 'I knows all that'.

There are several examples of the words and verb structures of this dialect here. Can you find them?

▼ Assignment 3

There is a dialect called Standard English which all English speakers can understand. It is used for any written documents that the writers want everyone to understand, which includes most newspaper articles, adverts, brochures and all official documents and school textbooks. It is also spoken on most radio and television broadcasts, especially for news bulletins.

In Standard English the sheep's 'They do never leave...' would be 'They never leave...' and 'I knows all that' would be 'I know all about that'. Can you put the 'sheep dialect' word structures you collected above into the form they would have in Standard English?

▼ Assignment 4

Can you think of any special dialect words or usages which are used in your locality or amongst people of your age-group?

▼ Assignment 5

The name 'sheep-pig' has been invented to describe a new sort of animal – a pig that wants to herd sheep. Many words come into the language like this. They are known as coinages.

'Sheep-pig' will not become a common word because there aren't any sheep-pigs around! But most coinages describe a new object which has become common, and so the word becomes part of the language.

Examples of recent coinages are: one-stop, laptop, high tech, mountain bikes, chatline.

In your groups, work out the meaning of these words and see how many other examples you can think of.

9:4 Madame Doubtfire

Daniel and Miranda are divorced and Daniel wants to spend more time with his children. Miranda wants someone to look after the children after school, and as Daniel, who is an actor, is out of work, it seems sensible for him to take the job. Miranda refuses to allow Daniel to do this, and so when Miranda advertises the post, Daniel makes sure he is the only applicant whose reply is received. He turns up for the interview dressed as Madame Doubtfire. He gets the job and has been working for Miranda for some time when the following takes place.

'The first time I knew that I'd married a madman', began Miranda, 'was my wedding day. I was nineteen. I wore a long, white frock and orange flowers in my hair. It was a glorious spring afternoon, with fluffy mountains of cloud moving across the bluest sky. Everyone we invited had come, except two miserable uncles I never really wanted anyway. It might have been a perfect day....'

'I've heard about this, I think,' said Christopher, doing his utmost to check her in the hope that his father would pick up his handbag and go home.

'Shh!' Natalie scolded. 'We're listening to the story!'

'The Registry Office was in the Town Hall. When I arrived, your father was already standing on the steps, watching a woman in the entrance to the supermarket next door.'

'I *know* I've heard this one', said Christopher, still hoping to forestall her.

'Be *quiet!*' Natalie hushed him fiercely.

'The woman was trying to give away kittens. Beside her was a cardboard box, and sweet little kitten ears and pink noses kept peeping over the top, and falling back. She had a home-made sign saying the kittens needed homes desperately, and any that hadn't been adopted by the time the supermarket closed that night would have to be put down.'

Natalie was sitting spell-bound. Her mother went on:

'I knew why Daniel was taking such an interest. His own cat had given birth to an enormous litter of kittens only eight weeks before, and he still hadn't managed to find

homes for any of them, even though we were about to go off on our honeymoon.'

'Where?' Lydia asked.

'The north of Scotland', Madame Doubtfire told her.

Miranda was astonished.

'How do you know that?'

There was a slightly uncomfortable pause before Madame Doubtfire explained.

'You remember those framed photographs stuffed away out of sight at the back of your wardrobe, dear? I tidied them last week, and couldn't help noticing one showed a fine looking figure of a man stealing a kiss from you over a beach café table.'

'But how did you guess that was my honeymoon?'

'Well!' Madame Doubtfire looked a little startled. 'Kissing in *public*, dear?'

'And how did you guess it was Scotland?'

'Recognised the cliffs, dear. And then the weather looked so very unpleasant....'

'Please!' Natalie begged. 'What about the poor kittens? Please tell about the kittens. *Please!*'

Distracted, Miranda took up the story as Christopher breathed again and Madame Doubtfire unobtrusively wiped sweat from her palms.

'As soon as he saw me, your father bounded down the steps. "Listen", he said. "I've just been talking to that woman. She had six kittens when she started. Apparently she stood there all day yesterday in the pouring rain, and all this morning through those nasty hail showers, and all this afternoon. Now she has only two kittens left, and a girl in the shop has promised to take one of those."'

It was clear from the expression on Natalie's face that this was a great load off her mind.

Miranda carried on.

'We were already late. I took his arm and we walked into the Town Hall. Everyone was waiting, and we were married straight away. Your father was in such a state, he dropped the ring twice.'

'You shouldn't need a weatherman to tell you which way the wind is blowing', Madame Doubtfire scolded her gently. 'You should have known to back out then, before it was all far, far too late.'

'So should he!' Miranda responded tartly.

'Anyhow, it would never have occurred to me to back out. I was so happy. I loved him, and I wanted him, and there we were, married at last. We stepped away from the Registrar's desk, and all our friends surged forward to hug us and kiss us and –'

She stopped short.

'And – ?'

'And – ?'

'And – ?'

Daniel forbore from joining the chorus. He knew, only too well, what was coming.

'And your father was gone!'

'Gone?'

'Gone?'

'Gone?'

'Gone! Disappeared. Nowhere to be seen. Slipped away. Vanished.'

'What did you *do*?'

'There wasn't much I could do, was there? I felt as if the skies had tumbled. I was embarrassed, miserable, humiliated and confused. My wedding had become a mockery. For all I knew, everything else was ruined as well.'

'It must have been *terrible* for you', said Lydia. She eyed Madame Doubtfire thoughtfully as she spoke.

Madame Doubtfire scowled, and taking this dark look for one of sympathy, Miranda carried on.

'I forced myself to pretend that nothing had happened. I sailed from guest to guest, laughing and chatting and tossing my hair. Whenever anyone slyly asked what had become of Daniel, I insisted he was bound to be back any moment, and was probably planning some wonderful surprise.'

'And was he?'

Lydia kept her cool, inscrutable eyes on Madame Doubtfire.

'Well ....' Miranda answered drily, 'it was a surprise ....'

'What *was* it?'

'Be *patient*. After about twenty minutes, when I was ready to *die* of embarrassment, the usher sidled up to my father and told him we would have to leave. There were other weddings, and we were clogging the foyer. So we all drifted out through the front door, on to the steps. And there was your father.'

'Where?'

'At the bottom of the steps, right in front of us. Just leaping off a number 27 bus. And in his arms there was a cardboard box.'

'The surprise!' shouted Natalie, glad that her father's honour was going to be restored at last.

Miranda glanced at her pityingly, before saying: 'Then, in front of *everyone,* with everyone *staring,* your father tucked the box under his arm, rushed up and grabbed me by the wrist. "Quick!" he hissed. "She'll be gone any minute!" He practically *shovelled* me down those steps. He bruised my arm. He tore my dress. In full view of everyone, he dragged me over to that poor woman who was still standing, forlorn and exhausted, outside the supermarket, desperate to find a home for her very last kitten. "Here!" he said to her. "These are for you!" And do you know what he did?'

Natalie writhed with impatience, desperate to be told.

'He lifted the flap of his cardboard box, and tipped a swirling, furry flurry into her box. The entire litter! Eight more sweet, adorable, vulnerable little kittens! The woman was appalled. Simply appalled! I thought that she was going to faint from the shock. She was so horrified she couldn't speak. And before I could say or do anything, Daniel had hauled me away, dragging me across the busy pavement and thrusting me up on the deck of some passing bus!'

How do we learn about characters?

What a character says

What a character does

What others say about him/her

▼ Assignment 1

1 What happened that was out of the ordinary on Daniel and Miranda's wedding day?
2 How did other people react to Daniel's behaviour on his wedding day? Look at the reaction of Lydia, the relatives and the lady with the cardboard box.
3 What did you think of his behaviour?
4 What do you learn about Miranda? Do you feel sorry for her? Explain why.
5 Now trace the outline of Daniel shown here and write around it what you learn about him as a character from what he says and does and from what other people say about him.

▼ Assignment 2

Write the next episode in the story that might have taken place after the wedding. Think about the following: imagine that you are Miranda. How would you feel about being dragged away before your wedding reception? If you were Daniel and you had had the problem of the kittens, what would you have done?

The other side of the coin

In the following extract, Miranda has sent Daniel a note that the children deliver. She says that the children are not going to be able to visit Daniel for the weekend as planned. Miranda thinks the children need new clothes and wants to take them shopping on Saturday – Daniel's day. This is the reaction of the family to this news:

'Phone her up!'
'Tell her!'
'Why *should* we miss all Friday night with you, and most of Saturday?'
'You can buy socks!'
'It's only fair!'
'It's your weekend, not hers.'
The voices, like the directives, gradually weakened. They, too, knew their mother.
'We could *ask*.'
'Yes, ask her!'
'She *might*. You never know.'
'We could *suggest* it.'
'Hint at it.'
'She won't let us, though.'
'She never does.'
'Never!'
'It isn't *fair*, is it?'
'No, it's not fair ....'
Daniel looked round at his children's faces, one raw with disappointment, two sourly miserable. He said to Lydia: 'You knew when you came in here, didn't you?'
She nodded, too dispirited even to dissemble.
'You, too?'

Christopher shrugged.

'But Natalie didn't.'

'She might as well have known', Christopher burst out. 'It happens practically every time. Whenever it's our turn to come to you, Mum manages to find some excuse. Rakes up some old great-aunt who hasn't sent a present in years, but suddenly can't last another weekend without having tea with us.'

'Or she buys tickets for something, and claims they only had seats left for that day.'

'Or she makes sure we have to come home to go to the doctor.'

'Or the dentist.'

'Or the optician.'

'Or we get to you hours late, because she's taking the car to be serviced.'

'Or we get picked up hours early because she's fetching it back.'

'We hardly ever see you.'

'And when we do, she's on the phone all the time.'

'Checking up on us, as if we were babies.'

'Checking up on you.'

In the next room the phone, like a timely haunting, began to ring. They sat, unnerved and silenced.

'I'll get it', Daniel said finally.

'Oh, no you won't', said Lydia. 'I can't stand any more today. *I'll get it*'...

It clearly wasn't anything quite so petty as socks this time, he suddenly realised. Her face was drawn and bloodless. She actually seemed to be swaying with rage. To his horror, he realised that this time, whatever it was her mother had rung up to say, it was so awful his daughter could not keep it to herself, even for a few moments. She was about to tell them all.

'Lydia!' he tried to stop her.

But it was too late. Already she had turned on her brother, whose humming drone dried to a faint, dried, staccato crackle at the mere sight of the look on his sister's face.

'The message was for you', she told him. 'It couldn't wait two hours till you got home. You had to be told now. She had to phone. You had to *know*.'

'Know what?' he asked her, terrified.

She took a deep breath.

'Lydia! No!'

It was as if it were a taste so bad she had to spit it out at once.

'The cat got at your hamsters. This time he really got at them. He tore them up. They're dead, both of them, Henry and Madge. She says she walked into the house to see mess and gore spread all over the rug.'

Her ghastly message off-loaded, Lydia turned away in tears.

Christopher bent over where he sat, on the floor, and buried his head in his arms. His shoulders heaved.

Natalie's fingers crept back in her ears.

Daniel looked round at his pale, miserable family.

'Good old Miranda', he muttered softly to himself. 'Another ruined teatime. So help me, one day I will slit her throat!'

This is taken from *Madame Doubtfire* by Anne Fine.

▼ **Assignment 3**

If you look back at the previous extract, you will see it was written from Miranda's point of view. This is written from Daniel's. Both extracts show evidence of bias. A lot of writing is biased because the people who write it have certain views.

As a group, discuss and write down what you think you learn about Miranda from this episode. Again, look at what she says and does and what the family say about her. Now try writing half a side explaining what Miranda is like and what you think of her.

▼ **Assignment 4**

Imagine you are the children in this story and that you have had enough of your parents' poor behaviour. You have to write them both a letter explaining how you would like them to improve. You are going to send them a joint letter because you think they are both pretty bad and need to be shown that each of them has faults. As a group, write the letter you would send.

9:5 Making Monsters (1)

> Frankie Stein is the daughter of a well-known scientist and one of four children – the rest are boys and are regarded as being very clever by the father. He does not think it is as important for Frankie to do well at school and does not take her interest in science seriously. She has managed to bribe her brother into giving her a portion of some jelly-like substance that he has stolen from his father's laboratory.

The Monster Garden

Once in my room again, I put the slide down on the table and looked round. Necessity, so they say, is the mother of invention. I hoped it would mother me.

My pot of African violets was standing in a saucer on the window sill. That would do. It was only a plain white saucer, slightly chipped, but we can't all be cradled in petrie dishes. My monster would have to rough it.

I washed and dried the saucer. Then I sterilized a needle in the flame of a match and pricked my thumb. I jabbed it harder than I meant to, and yelped. A scarlet bubble of blood appeared. I held my thumb over the saucer and squeezed.

I squeezed until my thumb ached, but the pool of blood, gleaming wetly in the sunlight, was disappointingly small. However, it would have to do. Carefully, I tipped the small grey lump into it.

Well! It quivered for a moment, like a jelly, and then lay still. It did not look alive.

Oh, well! I went to the Playhouse that evening with Hazel Brent and her parents. It was late when I got back. The sunlight had gone from the window sill. It was a hot night, dark and stuffy. I opened my window at the bottom without even noticing the saucer. My head was full of *My Fair Lady*.

'Da da dum dee dee', I sang as I went to bed. 'Aow, wouldn't it be luverly.'

I'd completely forgotten about my monster.

It thundered in the night. I woke up and lay watching the lightning cracking the sky. How vivid it was. It made me blink. I am not in the least frightened of thunderstorms, coming as I do from a scientific family. But I had never seen lightning like this before. It came leaping towards my window as if it wanted to come in. So quick, so bright! It hurt my eyes.

So I shut them, and turning to face the wall, went back to sleep. I didn't remember that my window was still open at the bottom. I did not think of my monster at all. I didn't dream.

In the morning, I woke to the sound of water flushing through the cistern. (My room is next to the bathroom.) I heard the door open and shut and footsteps going down the passage. David. Then I remembered.

I sprang out of bed and ran over to the window. The saucer on the sill had cracked and was oddly blackened, as if it had been rubbed with soot. There was nothing in it. David was right. I was too young to be trusted to look after things.

Oh well, never mind, I thought.

It must have been very windy in the night. The window sill was still wet and one or two seed pods had blown on to it. The carpet felt damp under my feet. Then I noticed that all the petals had gone from my African violets, and the few leaves that remained were tattered as if –

I stepped back. *As if something had bitten pieces out of them!*

Then I saw it.

It was in the far corner of the window sill. Squatting there. Not moving. It had grown during the night. Now it was the size of one of those pale toadstools you find at the roots of trees in Burners Wood. Silvery grey in colour, humped in the middle and thinning towards a transparent, crinkled edge. While I slept, the dark spot in the centre must have grown and split. It now had two red eyes and they were looking at me.

Nonsense, I told myself. But I did not move.

It twitched.

Slowly, horribly, it began to squirm and slither over the sill towards one of the seed pods. Then it stopped. A growth came out of its side, like a short fat tentacle, and pounced. The tentacle drew back into the body. I saw the seed pod twist and wriggle as the grey, half-transparent flesh simmered around it like thick stew. Then it was gone.

I bit my lip hard. Interesting, I told myself. Fascinating. Instructive.

I hated it. I wished it were dead. I wanted to scrape it into a tin, tip it down the loo and pull the handle.

There was a tin on my dressing table but I didn't even pick it up. I knew I couldn't do it. I can't kill things. Not even
105 things I dislike, like wasps and spiders and slugs. I'm too soft.

It is a flaw in my character, I suppose. David says that if you want to be a scientist, you cannot afford to be
110 squeamish. You have to train yourself to think of the good of mankind, and forget that some small, shivering creature may enjoy the sunlight as much as you do.

I have tried to train myself. I once
115 stood for ages in the garden, trying to be resolute and stamp on an ant. I raised my foot – but it was no good. The little ant looked so busy and happy, scurrying about in the green grass. I did not want my foot
120 to blot out its sun, like a thunderbolt descending. After all, it hadn't done me any harm.

So I didn't flush the monster down the loo. Instead, I pricked my thumb again, in
125 case it was thirsty.

'There you are', I said, pushing it off the sill into the saucer with the corner of an envelope. 'Drinkies.'

It quivered and blushed. No. It wasn't
130 blushing. It was the blood soaking up into the semi-transparent flesh. Ugh! It struck me then that perhaps it was not advisable to bring up a monster on my own blood. After all, I only had a limited supply. I
135 didn't want it to develop a taste for it.

This is taken from *The Monster Garden* by Vivien Alcock.

▼ Assignment 1

1 What preparations did Frankie make for the monster?
2 In your own words, explain what she did that a scientist with all the proper equipment might have done and what she did that was different.
3 Look at the description of the thunderstorm. Poets and playwrights sometimes describe things in nature or animals in a way that makes them sound human. This is called personification. Pick out one sentence that makes it sound as if this thunderstorm is a living thing and can behave like one.
4 Why do you think the author includes a thunderstorm in the story at this point? Can you think of another well-known story that this resembles?
5 How would you have felt about the monster if you had made it? Do you think you would have reacted in the same way as Frankie? Give reasons for your answer.
6 Read the whole passage and explain in your own words what you learn about Frankie Stein. Look carefully at lines 11–16, 24–35, 36–46, 47–51, 63–65, 103–to the end.

▼ Assignment 2

Imagine that you are Frankie Stein and you are keeping a scientific log of the experiment. Refer to the passage and in your own words fill in the entry she might make, based on the passage. For help with this refer to pages 24–7.

Assignment 3

Monster Garden was based on the story of *Frankenstein*, which was written in 1818. We are going to compare the two stories.

There is an extract below from *Frankenstein* about the creation of the monster. Get the best reader to read the passage aloud.

Remember, I am not recording the vision of a madman. The sun does not more certainly shine in the heavens than that which I now affirm is true. Some miracle might have produced it, yet the stages of the discovery were distinct and probable. After days and nights of incredible labour and fatigue, I succeeded in discovering the cause of generation and life: nay, more, I became myself capable of bestowing animation upon lifeless matter.

When I found so astonishing a power placed within my hands, I hesitated a long time concerning the manner in which I should employ it. Although I possessed the capacity of bestowing animation, yet to prepare a frame for the reception of it, with all its intricacies of fibres, muscles, and veins, still remained a work of inconceivable difficulty and labour. I doubted at first whether I should attempt the creation of a being like myself, or one of simpler organization; but my imagination was too much exalted by my first success to permit me to doubt of my ability to give life to an animal as complex and wonderful as man. The materials at present within my command hardly appeared adequate to so arduous an undertaking, but I doubted not that I should ultimately succeed. I prepared myself for a multitude of reverses; my operations might be incessantly baffled, and at last my work be imperfect: yet when I considered the improvement which every day takes place in science and mechanics, I was encouraged to hope my present attempts would at least lay the foundations of future success. Nor could I consider the magnitude and complexity of my plan as any argument of its impracticability. It was with these feelings that I began the creation of a human being. As the minuteness of the parts formed a great hindrance to my speed, I resolved, contrary to my first intention, to make the being of a gigantic stature; that is to say, about eight feet in height, and proportionably large. After having formed this determination and having spent some months in successfully collecting and arranging my materials, I began...

It was on a dreary night of November that I beheld the accomplishment of my toils. With an anxiety that almost amounted to agony, I collected the instruments of life around me, that I might infuse a spark of being into the lifeless thing that lay at my feet. It was already one in the morning; the rain pattered dismally against the panes, and my candle was nearly burnt out, when, by the glimmer of the half-extinguished light, I saw the dull yellow eye of the creature open; it breathed hard, and a convulsive motion agitated its limbs.

How can I describe my emotions at this catastrophe, or how delineate the wretch whom with such infinite pains and care I had endeavoured to form? His limbs were in proportion, and I had selected his features as beautiful. Beautiful! Great God! His yellow skin scarcely covered the work of muscles and arteries beneath; his hair was of a lustrous black, and flowing; his teeth of pearly whiteness; but these luxuriances only formed a more horrid contrast with his watery eyes, that seemed almost of the same colour as the dun-white sockets in which they were set, his shrivelled complexion and straight black lips.

    The different accidents of life are not so changeable as the feelings of human nature. I had worked hard for nearly two years, for the sole purpose of infusing life into an inanimate body. For this I had deprived myself of rest and health. I had desired it with an ardour that far exceeded moderation; but now that I had finished, the beauty of the dream vanished, and breathless horror and disgust filled my heart…

    I beheld the wretch – the miserable monster whom I had created… Eyes, if eyes they may be called, were fixed on me. His jaws opened, and he muttered some inarticulate sounds, while a grin wrinkled his cheeks. He might have spoken, but I did not hear; one hand was stretched out, seemingly to detain me, but I escaped and rushed downstairs. I took refuge in the courtyard belonging to the house which I inhabited, where I remained during the rest of the night, walking up and down in the greatest agitation, listening attentively, catching and fearing each sound as if it were to announce the approach of the daemoniacal corpse to which I had so miserably given life.

    Oh! No mortal could support the horror of that countenance. A mummy again endued with animation could not be so hideous as that wretch. I had gazed on him while unfinished; he was ugly then, but when those muscles and joints were rendered capable of motion, it became a thing such as even Dante could not have conceived.

This is taken from *Frankenstein* by Mary Shelley

Fiction

▼ **Assignment 4**

After the passage has been read out, make a list of all the words you didn't know. Use a dictionary and write down their meanings. Now look at the *Monster Garden* extract again. Are there many words there you do not understand?

▼ **Assignment 5**

Look again at the extracts from *Monster Garden* and *Frankenstein*. As a group, answer the following questions:

1 Which extract is the more frightening to the group, and why?

2 Look at the language of the two extracts. *Monster Garden* was written in 1988 and *Frankenstein* was written in 1818. Make a list of the words or phrases in *Frankenstein* that you don't hear people use today – words like 'nay' or 'bestowing', and phrases like 'The sun does not more certainly shine in the heavens than that which I now affirm is true'.

3 What difference has the audience made to the way both these books were written? *Frankenstein* was written for an adult audience and *Monster Garden* for children.

▼ **Assignment 6**

Look at the traditional artist's impression of Frankenstein's monster here. Now look at the passage and try to spot where ideas for this creature have come from. Copy this picture into your book. Next to each typical 'Frankenstein's monster' characteristic, explain whether this was described in the book or has been added later. Who do you think added the extra description, and why?

9:6 Making Monsters (2)

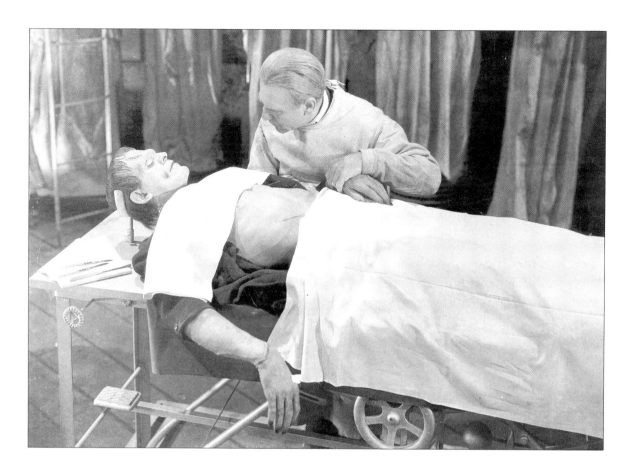

▼ Assignment 1

Look carefully at the film still above. Make a list of all the ideas that have come from the book. Then make a list of all the things that have come from elsewhere. Why do you think a film-maker changes things and sometimes puts in things that are not in the original story? Can any of you think of other films where this has happened?

▼ Assignment 2

Imagine that you are making the film of *Monster Garden*. You are busy preparing the storyboard for this film sequence.

Opposite is a miniature version of what a storyboard looks like. On a copy of this, fill in as many squares as you like to show how this would be filmed, paying particular attention to the lighting and sound effects that will be required. In each story square you need to give brief details of any dialogue spoken and any action that occurs.

STORYBOARD ////////////////

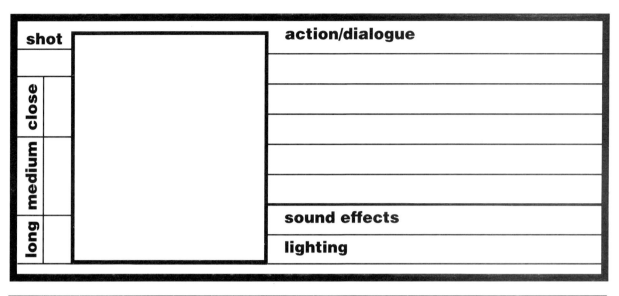

This sheet can be photocopied

9:7 Alice in Wonderland

> The Rabbit is eagerly looking for a fan and a pair of white kid gloves that he dropped earlier in the tale. Alice remembers he dropped them and hastily tries to help him find them.
> She runs quickly into the house at his request, and this is what happens next:

By this time she had found her way into a tidy little room with a table in the window, and on it (as she had hoped) a fan and two or three pairs of tiny white kid gloves: she took up the fan and a pair of the gloves, and was just going to leave the room, when her eye fell upon a little bottle that stood near the looking-glass. There was no label this time with the words 'DRINK ME', but nevertheless she uncorked it and put it to her lips. 'I know *something* interesting is sure to happen', she said to herself, 'whenever I eat or drink anything; so I'll just see what this bottle does. I do hope it'll make me grow large again, for really I'm quite tired of being such a tiny little thing!'

It did so indeed, and much sooner than she had expected: before she had drunk half the bottle, she found her head pressing against the ceiling, and had to stoop to save her neck from being broken. She hastily put down the bottle, saying to herself 'That's quite enough – I hope I shan't grow any more – As it is, I can't get out at the door – I do wish I hadn't drunk quite so much!'

Alas! It was too late to wish that! She went on growing, and growing, and very soon had to kneel down on the floor: in another minute there was not even room for this, and she tried the effect of lying down with one elbow against the door, and the other arm curled round her head. Still she went on growing, and as a last resource, she put one arm out of the window, and one foot up the chimney, and said to herself 'Now I can do no more, whatever happens. What *will* become of me?'

Luckily for Alice, the little magic bottle had now had its full effect, and she grew no larger: still it was very uncomfortable, and, as there seemed to be no sort of chance of her ever getting out of the room again, no wonder she felt unhappy.

'It was much pleasanter at home', thought poor Alice, 'when one wasn't always growing larger and smaller, and being ordered about by mice and rabbits. I almost wish I hadn't gone down that rabbit hole – and yet – and yet – it's rather curious, you know, this sort of life! I do wonder what *can* have happened to me! When I used to read fairy-tales, I fancied that kind of thing never happened, and now here I am in the middle of one! There ought to be a book written about me, that there ought! And when I grow up, I'll write one – but I'm grown up now', she added in a sorrowful tone; 'at least there's no room to grow up any more *here*.'

'But then', thought Alice, 'shall I *never* get any older than I am now? That'll be a comfort, one way – never to be an old

woman – but then – always to have lessons to learn! Oh, I shouldn't like *that*!'

'Oh, you foolish Alice!' she answered herself. 'How can you learn lessons in here? Why, there's hardly room for *you*, and no room at all for any lesson-books!'

And so she went on, taking first one side and then the other, and making quite a conversation of it altogether; but after a few minutes she heard a voice outside, and stopped to listen.

'Mary Ann! Mary Ann!' said the voice. 'Fetch me my gloves this moment!' Then came a little pattering of feet on the stairs. Alice knew it was the Rabbit coming to look for her, and she trembled till she shook the house, quite forgetting that she was now about a thousand times as large as the Rabbit, and had no reason to be afraid of it.

Presently the Rabbit came up to the door, and tried to open it; but, as the door opened inwards, and Alice's elbow was pressed hard against it, that attempt proved a failure. Alice heard it say to itself 'Then I'll go round and get in at the window.'

'*That* you won't!' thought Alice, and, after waiting till she fancied she heard the Rabbit just under the window, she suddenly spread out her hand, and made a snatch in the air. She did not get hold of anything, but she heard a little shriek and a fall, and a crash of broken glass, from which she concluded that it was just possible it had fallen into a cucumber frame, or something of the sort.

Next came an angry voice – the Rabbit's – 'Pat! Pat! Where are you?' And then a voice she had never heard before, 'Sure then I'm here! Digging for apples, yer honour!'

'Digging for apples, indeed!' said the Rabbit angrily. 'Here! Come and help me out of *this!*' (Sounds of more broken glass.)

'Now tell me, Pat, what's that in the window?'

'Sure, it's an arm, yer honour!' (He pronounced it 'arrum'.)

'An arm, you goose! Who ever saw one that size? Why, it fills the whole window!'

'Sure, it does, yer honour: but it's an arm for all that.'

'Well, it's got no business there, at any rate: go and take it away!'

This is taken from *Alice in Wonderland* by Lewis Carroll.

▼ **Assignment 1**

Look carefully at what has happened to Alice in the extract. After the adventure and before she went to sleep that night, she decided to write down what had happened to her in her diary. She had decided that one day she would include this in her autobiography, and so was careful to write a full account, giving details of how she felt at the time and what the Rabbit had said and done. Of course this has to be written in the past tense.

Alice spends a lot of time talking to herself, and you may be tempted to use the word 'said' a lot. Look at the poem below for some other possible words to use:

Poetry is fun

Teacher said ...
You can use
mumbled and muttered,
groaned, grumbled and uttered,
professed, droned or stuttered
... but *don't* use SAID!

You can use
rant or recite
yell, yodel or snort
bellow, murmur or moan
you can grunt or just groan
... but *don't* use SAID!

You can
hum, howl and hail
scream, screech, shriek or bawl
squeak, snivel or squeal
with a blood-curdling wail
... but *don't* use SAID!
SAID my teacher.

JUDITH NICHOLLS

9.8 M13 on Form

Told by X who never dares to give his/her name. The Cat's revenges are terrible and timeless.

'Books is comin,' yelled Mandy the Boot, blundering into the classroom in her father's size 12 army boots, and knocking Slasher Ormeroyd flying, which caused him to leap up with a mad roar and lurch to attack her, except that the Cat (Felix Delaney) paused in the middle of a poker game with Lia Tansy, Chinky Fred, and Tom Lightfinger to call out, 'Cool it, Slasher,' so that he hauled back his huge maulers for he always does what the Cat tells him. As we all do.

'What books?' enquired the Cat gently, for he was a great reader: crime and horror.

'A huge crate full. Old Perkins is turning 'em over an' oinkin' like a ma pig with piglets. There's hundreds.'

'Mr Perkins has comed back to us, doody, doody', crooned Daisy Chain, blue eyes beaming, bright hair bobbing. She loved Mr Perkins, and he was fond of her, not that he had much choice, M13 not being noted for its lovable characters. Mind you, we were all pleased to see him. He'd been absent on a course and the teacher they sent instead left in tears on Wednesday morning, making the rest of the week very tedious. The Headmaster took us. His name is Mr Bliss and it's a lie.

'That's great,' said Bat Pearson, resident genius. 'And about the books. We need new ones. Not that I read much fiction, haven't the time - she was wading through *A Study of Bog Burial in Scandinavia and Europe* (funny place to bury people, said Mandy) - but I like to keep Killer going and he can't stand *Little Women*.'

Killer, six feet two and growing, nodded, for Bat does all his work. In return he's her Minder. Most of us need one. M13 aren't popular in the school, not that they're popular out of it either.

'I like Enid Blyton', cried Hot Chocolate, the class prefect. 'I've read them all. Sir once said they'd made me what I am.'

'Belt up,' bellowed Hag Stevens from the doorway. 'Mr Perkins is on his way.' We were all so pleased to see him that we arranged ourselves nicely, looking keen and eager. And instead of sighing as he usually does at the sight of us, he smiled, which smoothed out all his wrinkles, like an American with a face lift.

'It's so nice to see you all again,' he said warmly, and as if that wasn't enough he was dressed in cords and check shirt. Where was his old chalky? What was up? 'As you know, I've been on a course, a language course, which I really enjoyed, and now I feel we can go forward with a new outlook.'

'A wha...?' asked Brain Drain, dim even by M13's standards.

'A new outlook on the rest of our year together. Speaking to you honestly, as your friend as well as teacher, that course came just in the nick of time, for I's begun to despair at the thought of us struggling and drowning together ...'

'I wunt let yer drown, Sir,' interrupted Brain Drain, breathing hard, for uttering more than two words was always difficult. 'I kin swim.'

'Quite,' Sir agreed. 'Now let's see if my old friends are all here ... Abdullah, Asra, Brian ...'

Killer and Slasher were despatched to carry in the heavy crate, Bat Lia and Mandy to organise the class resource centre. The rest of the school has a central area, but it was decided that M13 should just keep theirs in the classroom, after Tom Lightfinger flogged all the cassette players and musical instruments

to some teenage pals to start a group.

'Any 'orror comics or girlie mags?' Slasher asked Killer hopefully.

'No, shurrup. The Cat looks after that side, and y'know he don't think it right for old Perkins to learn about such things. Not at his age.'

Eventually all the splendid new books were arranged and the classroom transformed. Mr Perkins had done well, something for everyone: *Dr Seuss* for Brain Drain and Daisy and the Heap, *War and Peace* for Bat, *An Anthology of Horror* for the Cat. He beamed at us all.

'Yes, you shall soon get at them, but first something new for a new day. Has anyone a poem for me? A suitable poem, mind, Ormeroyd.'

A mind-boggling hush fell for we always turned to the Cat or Bat or Mandy to represent us on these occasions and they all three despised poetry (wet, useless, boring). And then Brain Drain lumbered to his feet.

'I know one about an ickle worm.' And he recited it while Sir grinned like a maniac.

'Jolly good,' he cried. 'They told me it would work. Good old M13. Don't let me down. Surely you must know a poem, Beatrice.'

Bat stood up, grimacing horribly, embarrassed. 'The only one I know is a dead boring one from Horace, about a smelly, skinny youth. Dates back to my classical hang-up last year. Sorry. Will that do?'

Sir nodded, and the Latin phrases hung in the classroom already quite well-known for its language. Killer smiled approvingly. His Bat was doing well even if no one could understand a word of it. And Tom

Lightfinger got up, brick red. 'Know one about a dicky bird,' he said, head down. 'Learnt it in the Infants.' One by one M13 made their offerings, the Cat last, with the lyrics of an obscure cult rock group.

A week later anyone walking into M13's classroom, and most people preferred not to, would have had to weave their way through poems everywhere – on the walls, on the windows, standing in displays, hanging on string, swinging in mobiles, for M13 had taken to poetry, writing poems, reading poems, reciting poems, illustrating poems. Mr Perkins had seen a miracle in his lifetime and walked on air. The school grapevine had it that the class had either gone barmy or had reformed at last. Actually, it was, as usual, the Cat.

Shoulders hunched, black glasses, white face, he said, 'I want old Perkins to be happy. De poetry mikes him happy. So we get with de poetry. See?' We saw.

When it wasn't poetry, it was stories. M13 went book-mad, reading all of the time all over the place, even walking round the playground reading, with Killer and Slasher there to settle anyone foolish enough to find it funny. Those who understood what those squiggles on a page meant helped those who didn't.

So occupied were we, we didn't notice that the school's big issue was now Conservation. A famous celebrity had addressed the school subject and projects mushroomed everywhere. But it wasn't until a very pretty lady came to tell the school of the plight of a butterfly that was about to die out unless money could be raised to provide a Nature Reserve where it could breed that M13 realised it was needed.

'Dat poor icle utterfly,' muttered Brain Drain, moved.

Now despite everything: lies, thefts, vandalism, dishonesty, cheating, bullying, greed, truancy, you name it, M13's got it: despite all these or as well as, M13 has Heart. Disasters, we weep over disasters. Earthquakes bring contributions from us faster than anyone. Tom Lightfinger has been known to pinch the Save the Children pennies bottle from the corner shop to contribute to the class's gift. So when the very pretty lady said there was to be a prize for the best school contribution – a silver medal – and a framed poem about a butterfly written by the very pretty lady herself for the best class collection, there could be no doubt about it. M13 intended to get that prize, that poem on their wall.

No one needed to tell M13 about fund-raising. We have a natural talent for it: begging, gambling, sponsoring, busking, collecting, blackmailing, grovelling, stealing, shop-lifting, extorting, bullying, even selling, we went about it all in the way that suited each of us best. Yet in the final week but one, the grapevine informed the Cat that Hadley Grove School were the favourites, their rich parents being plushier than ours.

Mr Perkins was heard to remark with pleasure on the industry of his class, most pleased, most pleased. Reading, writing and money-raising thrived. An experienced teacher, though, every Friday he collected in the books that had worked the miracle (he thought) and checked them. That Friday only Bat's was missing and she promised faithfully etc. Mr Perkins went home. Happy.

On Monday morning all the shelves were empty. All the books had disappeared. So had every leaflet, magazine, poster and map in the resources area. His face sagged back into all those wrinkles, and he took the register, all present, except for Brain Drain.

'Right, what have you lot done with them?' He didn't look at all like that nice Mr Perkins. He looked more like Hanging Judge Jeffreys.

'Delaney, what have you organised?'

'Nothing, Sir.' The Cat at a loss, for once. 'Honest.'

'You don't know what honesty is, Delaney.'

But the cat stood firm; it was nothing to do with him nor anyone else that he knew of.

'Then, Lightfinger, it just has to be you.'

'No, no, no. I liked the books. They just took what I was half-way in the middle of and I haven't finished. And I dint read the ending first, for once.'

'Hard luck,' snapped Mr Perkins, cruelly.

And the door crashed open as the vast, shaggy head of Brain Drain appeared first, then the rest of him, waving a fistful of money.

'For the utterfly pome, Mr Perkins. For de pome. We win it now, won't we? Look at all de lolly. And I did it for you, Mr Perkins, becos you give me all dem pomes and I love pomes now.'

'Brian, look at me and stop gabbling. Where did you get that money? And do you know what's happened to all our books?'

'I've conserved our books. Dey'll go on f'ever an'ever. An'dey gived me lolly for' em. Look.'

'But how?' groaned Mr Perkins.

Brain Drain was panting like an old train at full steam ahead. 'Me auntie Mave. Cleanin' after school, an' she give me this dustbin bag an' I put 'em all in an' took 'em to our church for rebikin'...'

'For what?' Mr Perkins looked as if he was going demented.

'Recycling,' translated Bat.

'An' they said what a good cause, and gived me money an' we'll win the pome now, wun't we?' he beamed. He sat down and then bobbed up again in the heavy silence. 'Mr Perkins, Sir?'

'Yes, Brian?' came a low moan.

'I conserved them books and the utterfly, dint I?'

'Oh, Brian, you did, you did.'

After a long time the Cat spoke, and for possibly the first time in his life his voice was full of pity.

'M13. Listen. De kindness, get it? From now on we are going to be kind to Mr Perkins.'

How M13 visited the recycling plant, rescued all the books (not very suitable anyway, they said), was spotted by the Mayor, also visiting, got its picture in all the papers (such keen children), won the school medal and the butterfly poem (more pictures in the papers – what fine, hardworking children, an example to others), so that at last Brain Drain could hang the pome on the wall – except they'd gone on to computer games by then – and as usual were hated bitterly by the rest of the school (good, hardworking, boring children) is another story.

Gene Kemp

Fiction

ACKNOWLEDGEMENTS

The author would like to thank the following for their invaluable help;

The staff and pupils of Queen Elizabeth, Cambria School, Carmarthen.
The Head of English and pupils at Cooper School, Bicester.

The author and publishers would like to thank the
following for permission to reproduce copyright material:

Adidas Ltd for advertisement; Alton Towers for map of Alton Towers; Anderson Press for extract from *Conrad the Factory-Made Boy* by Christine Nostlinger; ASA (The Advertising Standards Authority Ltd) for advertisement; Basil Blackwell for extract from *Themes in Design & Technology Flight* by John Jones, 1987; British Rail for Young Person's Railcard advertisement; BUAV (British Union for the Abolition of Vivisection) for advertisement; CIBA Geigy Pharmaceuticals for 'Triac' advertisement; Dinosaur Museum, Dorset, for their advertisement; The Diving Museum and Shipwreck Centre, Weymouth, for their advertisement; *The Early Times* for 'A Trio of Tortoise Tales'; Elefriends, the Elephant Protection Group for advertisement; Faber and Faber Ltd for 'M13 on Form' by Gene Kemp from *In A Class of Their Own* by Barbara Ireson, and for 'Teacher Said' by Judith Nichols from *Magic Mirror & Other Poems for Children,* 1985; Victor Gollancz Ltd for extract from *The Sheep-Pig* by Dick King-Smith; Hamish Hamilton Ltd for extract from *Madam Doubtfire* by Anne Fine; Rosemary Joseph for 'Baking Day'; Methuen Children's Books for extract from *The Monster Garden* by Vivien Alcock; NSPCC (The National Society for the Prevention of Cruelty to Children) for advertisement; PGL Young Adventure Ltd for Superb Activity Holidays Ad; Pluto Press for extract from *Acid Rain* by Steve Elsworth, 1984; Samual French Ltd for extract from *Dick Whittington* by John Morley; J Salman Ltd for Hardy's Birthplace card; Shepheard-Walwyn Publishers Ltd for extract for their advertisement, © Tank Museum; The Sea Chef Restaurant, Weymouth, for their advertisement; The Sea-life Centre, Dorset, for leaflets; Unicef for advertisement; Ward Lock Educational for extract from *Complete Book of Home Crafts* by Pamela Westland; West Country Tourist Board for Hardy's Birthplace Leaflet; Westers Bistro Bar, Weymouth, for their advertisement; Weymouth Tourist Information Centre for map of Weymouth; Kit Wright for 'Useful Person'.

It has not been possible to trace all copyright holders.
The publishers would be glad to hear from any unacknowledged
sources at the first opportunity.

We would also like to thank the following for permission to reproduce photographs on the pages noted:

Barnaby's Picture Library pp 48, 49 (bottom), 50; Carcanet Press p 74; Greg Cullen p 56;
Richard Firstbrook pp 18, 19, 20, 21; B Gale pp 51, 58 (bottom right), 59 (top left);
Hutchinson Picture Library p 49 (top), 84 (right and top left); Peter Johnson (bottom right);
The Kobal Collection p116; Chris Ridgers 88, 89, 80; Woodmansterne Ltd
pp 58 (top right), 59 (top left and bottom).